THE BATTLE FOR
Crete

SEA BATTLES IN CLOSE-UP · 5

THE BATTLE FOR
Crete

S. W. C. PACK

Naval Institute Press

First published 1973

Dedicated to all those nations of the British Commonwealth who rallied with Britain to fight the aggressors in World War II, and with gratitude for their prompt, unfailing, and loyal support. In those critical dark days of 1941, typified by such setbacks as the Battle for Crete, they courageously stood by Britain when she was virtually alone. Those many lives so gallantly given in the cause of freedom were not given in vain.

Library of Congress Catalog Card No. 72-86341

ISBN 0–87021–810–7

Published and distributed in the United States of America by the Naval Institute Press

Printed in Great Britain

Contents

DIAGRAMS

Preface

The loss of Crete in May 1941, after a battle of only a few days, appeared as a crowning disaster to the British people who had faced one setback after another, mitigated only by Cunningham's decisive successes at Taranto and Matapan, and Wavell's momentous sweep across Cyrenaica.

The battle for Crete will remain a matter for discussion as long as the study of history continues its fascination for mankind. The issue was narrow; the attack was expected for weeks before the event; the assault was entirely airborne; the British determination to hang on to Crete despite lack of air power was not in doubt. Yet the result was conclusive after less than twelve days of resolute fighting by both sides. And the losses by air, land, and sea were enormous.

The case for the defence was cogently stated by the Prime Minister, Mr Winston Churchill, in the House of Commons June 10, 1941, a few days after the loss of Crete. In rebutting the doctrine that resistance should be offered only when success is certain, he said:

'The choice was whether Crete should be defended without effective air support or should the Germans be permitted to occupy it without opposition . . . there are some arguments which deserve to be considered before you can adopt the rule that you have to have a certainty of winning at any point, and if you have not got it beforehand clear out.

'The whole history of war shows the fatal absurdity of such a doctrine. Again and again it has been proved that fierce and stubborn resistance even against heavy odds and under exceptional conditions of local disadvantage is an essential element of victory.'

This book emphasises the naval contribution to the battle, but a brief account of the continuing events in Crete (the assault and the defence) is given to provide a balanced narrative. It is hoped that the

7

maps will assist the reader in his comprehension of the difficulties inherent in the great distances involved. For the student of statistics and technical data, there are several appendices and tables providing information about the ships, men, defences, bomb attacks, numbers evacuated, losses, lessons learnt, and the relative performance of various types of aircraft in use, ending with a comparison of destroyer fuel consumption at various speeds, which was such a crucial feature of the unceasing naval operations.

I am indebted to M. Brennan, Esq, of the Imperial War Museum, for help with the illustrations, which unless otherwise credited were all supplied by them; to J. D. Brown, Esq, of the Naval Historical Branch for help generally; to G. White, Esq, of the Britannia RN College Library for assistance with books; and to Miss Freda Busby for her magnificent typing and manuscript corrections. Above all I owe gratitude to my wife for her endless encouragement and help.

Blossom's Pasture,   S. W. C. Pack
Devon, 1972

CHAPTER ONE

Assault from the Sky

TUESDAY MAY 20TH

The story begins on a sunny morning at Maleme in the beautiful island of Crete on Tuesday May 20th, 1941. It was calm and clear; a deep blue sky overhead, and a visibility of twenty miles to seaward. The Royal Naval Air station, close to the village of Maleme, lay on the north coast, not far from the western end of this elongated island which is roughly a rectangle 150 miles by 30 miles. It is important to realise how effectively Crete acts as a barrier to the Aegean Sea, like a detached breakwater, with the Kithera and Antikithera channels at the western end, and the Kaso and Scarpanto straits at the eastern end. Greece, a hundred or so miles north and north-west of Crete, was now occupied by the Germans, since the British, unable to maintain adequate strength, had withdrawn at the end of April 1941 after a campaign of only a few weeks in support of the Greeks. Many of those British troops, mainly Australian and New Zealand, had been evacuated to Crete to supplement the British garrison, but in numerous cases they were without adequate weapons and equipment. On the north coast, Suda, the main port of Crete, suffered from severe limitations in the unloading of stores, owing to the absence of deep water berths alongside. It was 420 sea miles by the shortest route from Alexandria and nearer 500 by the west-about route. German-held Piraeus, almost due north of Maleme and Suda, was only 170 sea miles away from Crete (see Diag 1 and 2).

Daily since May 14th there had been 'softening up' bombing attacks on the airfield at Maleme, as also on the smaller airfields at Retimo and Heraklion, 30 and 60 miles farther east respectively. Tuesday May 20th was no exception. German aircraft arrived soon after 06.00hrs and for the next hour or two there were as usual the shrieking whine of dive bombers, the crunch of exploding bombs, the rattle of cannon from fighters, and the comforting blast of anti-aircraft fire from the defence posts to the south and east of the airfield.

By 08.00hrs it became clear that the air attacks this day were of a more savage intensity than earlier ones. Shortly afterwards, during the first lull in the bombing, gliders were seen swooping down to the west of the Maleme airfield, and also on both sides of the head-quarters at Canea three miles eastward of Maleme. The skies became full of large silvery shapes with long tapering wings passing silently above the heads of the defenders, in marked contrast with the deafening racket that had accompanied the preceding bombing phase. And now the roar of anti-aircraft fire re-opened. One or two of the gliders twisted and turned; some crashed. In general the body of them carried relentlessly on, unperturbed by the relatively small anti-aircraft defence, and quite unopposed by any form of British air offensive, for all fighters had been neutralised or withdrawn during the preceding days. Even one Hurricane could have created tremen-dous havoc. As the gliders landed, Germans sprang out in all directions, armed with mortars, machine-guns, and hand grenades: wave upon wave.

There was scarcely a break between the arrival of the last of the hundred or so gliders and the appearance of slow-moving Ju52s* overhead, loaded with German paratroopers. In many cases the troop carriers were painted black with yellow noses. In a moment, hundreds of figures attached to parachutes of different colours, red, yellow, green, blue, and black, could be seen descending from various heights. In addition to troops, the planes were dropping field guns, anti-tank guns, ammunition, food, and medical supplies. The dangling figures, fifteen from each transport, and later in greater numbers up to forty, wore camouflage overalls and crash helmets, and their descent to the ground took anything up to 20 seconds, during which many were killed outright if they were unlucky enough to drop close to defended positions. Some landed far from the defenders, and quickly moved towards a previously agreed rallying point where there was plenty of cover in olive groves or vineyards. Domination of the air by the Germans played a crucial part, for not only was the sky full of their aircraft, giving them a clear picture of the land fighting, and an awareness of in-cipient counter-attacks by the defenders, but fighters were able also

* See Appendix I (B) (2)

Diagram I. (*Opposite*) Crete as a barrier to the Aegean Sea.

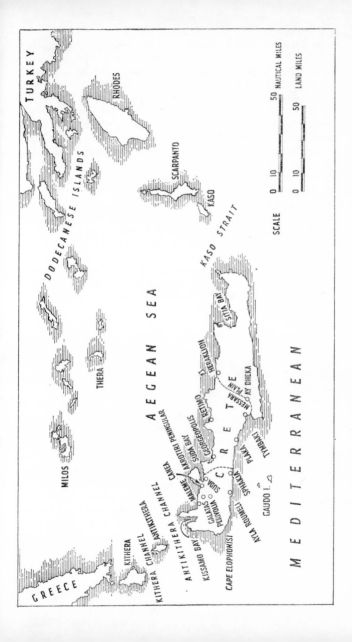

to neutralise such developments and pin defending troops to their cover.

The British had known since early May that a vast airborne assault on Crete was being prepared by the German Luftwaffe, and it was believed that German eyes were turning also to Cyprus and farther eastward to Iraq. The defenders were not therefore taken by surprise on Tuesday May 20th, though powerless to strengthen defences appreciably, owing to rival claims elsewhere and the fact that heavy weapons and fighting equipment had had to be abandoned during the recent evacuation from Greece. The general opinion was that Crete could be held, provided that the assault was airborne only. This was based on the principle that the Germans would be unable to land heavy guns, tanks, vehicles, and reinforcements, except by sea. It was therefore expected that they might attempt a seaborne landing in support of the airborne assault, the prevention of which would become the Royal Navy's rôle. In view of the possibility of continuous German and Italian air attacks around Crete, and the absence of any substantial Royal Air Force strength closer than 500 miles, together with the added chance of a sortie from the Italian fleet, it was evident that the Navy's task would be stretched to the limits.

In addition to shore-based air cover around Crete being non-existent, the Navy's only available carrier HMS *Formidable* (in which the author was serving) was now lying at Alexandria, with her complement of sixteen Fulmar fighter aircraft reduced to barely four, having suffered increasing losses during the intensely active period following her arrival in the Mediterranean on March 10th, shortly before the battle of Matapan.

At the moment of the intensified bombing which initiated the 'softening up' phase for Crete, there had been at the RN Maleme airfield under the command of Commander G. H. Beale, RN (later Captain DSO, OBE), three Gladiators and three Fulmars of the Fleet Air Arm, together with three Royal Air Force Hurricanes which had come from Greece. The aircraft and the crews were both virtually unfit for further sustained effort, nevertheless Fleet Air Arm pilots Lieutenant-Commander Alan Black and Lieutenant R. A. Brabner, together with a Royal Air Force Squadron-Leader Edward Howell (flying a Hurricane for the first time in his life), against almost overwhelming odds, shot down six Messerschmitts. On the following day forty German planes were attacked by two Hurricanes, after which final effort no serviceable aircraft existed at Maleme, and the pilots were sent back to Egypt. Beale remained at Maleme with the maintenance crews to organise defence.

Details of the military dispositions in preparation for the German assault, and an account of the blow by blow fighting on shore, form no part of the story of the sea battle for Crete. Nevertheless, brief coverage will be given as the narrative proceeds. Both sides were optimistic, and the battle ashore was one of the bloodiest encounters of the war. The result was in doubt for some days, and intense resolution and bravery were shown on both sides. The first attacks were borne almost entirely by the New Zealand Division, and the toughness and stubbornness of the defence came as a surprise to the Germans, who had hoped to be in possession of Maleme airfield by the end of the first day. In the following days the Germans were greatly concerned at their own losses and lack of progress, and allowed no rebuff to lead to any diminution of effort, but rather to an intensification of the assault with more and more airborne reinforcements arriving under the German domination of the skies, combining aerial attacks upon the strong points, and paratroop movements which attempted to isolate pockets of resistance. Their aerial view of the scene, denied to the pinned-down defenders, proved to be of the greatest tactical importance.

It was not until April 30th that Major-General B. C. Freyberg, VC, CB, CMG, DSO, had assumed command of the British and Imperial forces in Crete. Less than three weeks later the airborne assault began. Although British intelligence had knowledge of German intentions, it was still uncertain whether the assault would be airborne, seaborne, or both. This fact severely limited Freyberg's plans for defence, for in the event he had to allow flexibility so as to be prepared for all three.

The German plans were for air landings of 13,000 troops to take place at Maleme on the forenoon of the first day, and at Retimo and Heraklion that afternoon. These were to be followed by mainly seaborne landings of 9,000 mountain troops with guns, tanks, and heavy stores, transport being provided by steamships and caiques. The prospect that these might be escorted by units of the Italian fleet would give Admiral Cunningham's fleet something more to think about. We shall read of his preparations in Chapter Three.

CHAPTER TWO

The Deteriorating British Position in the Mediterranean 1940-1941

To understand Britain's defence in the battle for Crete, and more especially (from the point of view of this book) the part played by the Royal Navy in that epic story, it is necessary to follow briefly the events during the previous eleven months and to note particularly the character of the Commander-in-Chief of the British Mediterranean Fleet.

Admiral Sir Andrew B. Cunningham, GCB, DSO, known affectionately as ABC, was determined to gain command of the sea and to keep it. His concept of sea power was clear: it was the ability to use the sea wherever British and Imperial interests lay, and to overcome any opposition that disputed those interests. If the enemy should have a preponderance of ships then it was ABC's aim to neutralise such a situation at the first opportunity so as to discourage interference with the transport of British ships and supplies. He had always had a great regard for the Royal Navy's traditional responsibility of conveying the British Army safely to wherever it was ordered to go. At the same time, his own fleet must be able to stop the transport of enemy troops and supplies. Never to be forgotten is his signal on May 22nd, 1941, on a day when his fleet had suffered, at the hand of overwhelming enemy air superiority, losses which were almost disastrous. The signal ran:

'Stick it out. Navy must not let Army down. No enemy forces must reach Crete by sea.'

This signal was of course in the same vein as his frequently expressed warning that 'It takes the Navy three years to build a ship. It would take three hundred to rebuild a tradition.' It was inspiration and leadership of this calibre that enabled his fleet to meet and survive the supreme test of Crete.

The entry of Italy on the side of Germany on June 11th, 1940, followed by the collapse of France, had gravely compromised the British situation in the Mediterranean. The Italian Navy had a marked material preponderance, her ships being generally newer, faster, and better armed, compared with those of the British Mediterranean Fleet. By firm persuasion and supreme tact throughout a period of painful and difficult negotiations, Cunningham, with the aid of his staff and the captains of HM ships in the Fleet, had been able to arrange for the immobilisation of the French warships under Vice-Admiral Godfroy at Alexandria, so that there was no danger of their falling into enemy hands. Also the British Mediterranean Fleet had been strengthened and its main base shifted eastwards from Malta to Alexandria.

Malta had been one of Cunningham's main concerns and he was determined to hold the island that had been the British Navy's principal base for almost a century and a half. Convoys were run to Malta with provisions from Alexandria, and reverse convoys carried to Alexandria much needed equipment and technical services which were becoming necessary for the repair and maintenance of the Fleet in this relatively ill-equipped base. The Commander-in-Chief also regarded these convoys as providing tempting opportunities for the Italian Fleet to put to sea. This in fact happened off Calabria on July 9th, 1940, when it appeared that a fleet action was imminent against two Italian battleships, twelve cruisers, and a large number of destroyers. The Italian Fleet flagship was hit by the *Warspite*'s accurate firing at a range of 13 miles, and the action was immediately broken off by the Italian admiral.

Cunningham had informed the First Sea Lord that he must have at least one other battleship, additional to the modernised *Warspite*, that could fire at a range comparable with the two new Italian 35,000-ton, 15in battleships *Littorio* and *Vittorio Veneto*. He further stressed the vital need for one of Britain's new armoured aircraft carriers and the need for fighter protection for the Fleet and convoys when close to the enemy shore. As a result, the modernised old battleship *Valiant*,* sister ship of the *Warspite*, and the new armoured aircraft carrier *Illustrious*, together with two newly converted anti-aircraft cruisers *Calcutta* and *Coventry*, joined his fleet in September 1940.

These additions did much to reduce the material superiority enjoyed by the Italians, and the difference had been further reduced on the night of November 11th, 1940, when *Illustrious* approached to

* In which Midshipman Prince Philip of Greece was serving

within 170 miles of Taranto and flew off naval aircraft to attack the Italian Fleet lying in harbour. One battleship, the *Cavour*, was sunk by torpedo, and two others, the new *Littorio* and the older *Duilio*, were damaged and put out of action. This raid weakened Italian morale considerably. It was a great distinction for the Fleet Air Arm with its gallant band of young pilots, observers, and gunners, many of whom, though as yet relatively inexperienced, had at last come into their own with a magnificent success.

With a view to gaining control of the Eastern Mediterranean, Mussolini treacherously invaded Greece on October 28th, 1940, and met with an unexpected set-back. Within three months Italian forces were being driven back into Albania by the Greeks, thus giving Hitler an excuse for a German thrust through the Balkans, his idea being to neutralise Turkey and Greece, and threaten British dominance in the Eastern Mediterranean. Hitler also sent his well-trained Fliegerkorps X to stiffen the Italian Regia Aeronautica in Sicily. This was to have a profound effect later in increasing Axis air superiority over the narrow waters between Sicily and Tunisia. To the dangers from Italian high level bombing was now added the deadly dive bombing from German Stukas.

The Italian Navy of 1940 was excellent in respect of speed, armament, and manoeuvres, but it suffered from two serious defects. One was the absence of any experience of night fighting, and the other was the fact that it possessed no aircraft carriers. Mussolini had ruled against the construction of carriers, accepting the view of his Air Force that all ships in the central Mediterranean, including carriers, would be at the mercy of their shore-based high level bombers. The blow at Taranto made him rue his decision, and the battle of Matapan, March 1941, caused him to reverse it; but it was too late. Italy's only carrier the *Aquila* was destroyed before final completion.

On December 9th, 1940, supported from the sea by Cunningham's fleet, General Sir Archibald Wavell had launched his brilliant offensive at Sidi Barrani. By December 15th all Egypt was free of Italian troops. By February 9th, 1941, the British Army of the Nile stood before El Agheila,* having advanced westward six hundred miles and taken 130,000 prisoners.

On January 10th, when Cunningham's fleet met a fast eastbound British convoy in the Sicilian narrows, a strong formation of Ju87

* See map of Eastern Mediterranean p 25

and Ju88* dive bombers with fighter escort concentrated on the *Illustrious*. Though very seriously damaged from six hits, she managed to reach Malta and subsequently Alexandria, though in need of extensive and fundamental repairs which would be carried out in the United States. On January 11th the cruiser *Southampton* was dive-bombed and had to be abandoned and sunk. The presence of the Luftwaffe in Sicily was now seriously hampering movements of British ships.

The neutralisation of the *Illustrious* was a grievous loss, but the new carrier *Formidable* was available in the South Atlantic and arrived at Alexandria on March 10th, 'having (due to a wreck) been squeezed through the canal with literally no more than a few feet to spare on either side'.

Cunningham was relieved to have once again a modern carrier available. In referring to new methods for countering the German dive bombers he wrote that he intended to 'make the destroyer screen put up an umbrella barrage over a particular ship, probably the carrier' (always the centre of attraction). 'I am also going to have twelve fighters in the air over the fleet.'

Admiral Raeder urged the Italian Navy to increase activity and to attack British communications in the Aegean in order to protect the German southern flank. Nevertheless the Italians were loath to expose their warships. A shortage of oil fuel also tended to keep their fleet in harbour. Towards the end of March, however, Admiral Iachino in his new flagship the *Vittorio Veneto* made a sortie eastwards with a powerful fleet. He was unfortunate in having practically no air support, though it had been promised by the Germans. Cunningham had smartly put to sea when the Italian fleet was reported, and thanks to the presence of the *Formidable* and her aircraft which provided him with reconnaissance reports, torpedo bomber strikes, and fighter defence, had been able to damage Iachino's battleship; and in a night action for which the Italians were totally unprepared, Cunningham's fleet had sunk three heavy Italian cruisers and two destroyers. In addition to the torpedo strikes by *Formidable*'s Albacores, similar strikes had been launched by Fleet Air Arm Swordfish from Maleme in Crete, and high level bombing attacks by RAF Blenheims from Menidi in Greece.

This victory came as a much-needed boost to British morale. At the same time it resulted in a great stimulation of German air activity
* See Appendix I (B) (3)

which was soon to neutralise what little air defence could now be provided by the Royal Air Force in Greece and in the environs of Crete. The air defence provided by the *Formidable*'s fighters, and the concentration of the anti-aircraft guns of all ships in an umbrella barrage, were an effective defence for the fleet, but only while aircraft lasted and anti-aircraft ammunition continued to be available.

The transport of British troops from Egypt to Greece ('Operation Lustre') began on March 5th and continued for three weeks during which 25 merchantmen were bombed and sunk, mainly after arrival in harbour. British fighter strength was too limited to give much protection. During this time, Rommel's Afrika Korps was being strengthened in Libya through Tripoli.

On March 30th Rommel made his lightning strike in Cyrenaica. In two weeks Wavell's depleted Army of the Nile was driven back to the Egyptian frontier, losing once more the whole of Cyrenaica (Benghazi, Derna, and Bardia), except for Tobruk. The presence of hostile airfields in the bulging coastline of Cyrenaica, with Rommel poised to advance into Egypt, was now to add increasing menace to the retention of British sea power. Cunningham's response was to take his whole fleet to sea, and steam a thousand miles to the westward.

In the early hours of April 21st the British fleet subjected the harbour works of Tripoli to bombardment, supplemented by bombing and strafing attacks by *Formidable*'s aircraft. A supply ship was run into Malta. Five days earlier, four British destroyers had annihilated an Italian convoy of five ships off Sfax in Tunisia. Surface warships were unable to remain in Malta, but periodic re-inforcements by Hurricanes together with a few British submarines permitted continued use of the island for offensive purposes against Rommel's supply lines to Tripoli.

The German blitzkrieg on Greece opened on April 6th, 1941, with a force of overwhelming strength, backed by a thousand aircraft. Within two weeks Greece had collapsed and the situation for the British rapidly deteriorated; the danger of losing all the 58,000 British troops soon became obvious. Evacuation from eight different harbours was undertaken by Cunningham's light forces from April 24th–29th, and although guns and equipment had to be left behind, 51,000 men were taken off. These were sent to Egypt, except for 21,000 who were landed as reinforcements for the British garrison in Crete. Though Britain still held the sea, the Germans now had practically undisputed supremacy in the air, and were in full control of Rumania, Bulgaria, Greece, and of many of the Aegean islands. They were also at the gates of Egypt; but Crete remained a British threat to the German southern flank, and the peril in which it stood was all too clear.

Strategically, 'Operation Lustre' appeared to have been unwise, resulting in near disaster. The political need to support Greece had however been unavoidable.

In view of the urgent need for reinforcements, it was decided once more to attempt the direct eastward passage for a convoy ('Operation Tiger'), carrying tanks, guns, vehicles, and planes. At the same time the old modernised battleship *Queen Elizabeth* and the cruisers *Naiad* and *Fiji* were to join Cunningham's fleet that had travelled westward from Alexandria to meet them. Thanks, miraculously, to sandstorm, fog, mist, low cloud, and a tremendous fleet barrage during the only clear spell in the period of May 6th–12th, losses were small; 238 tanks and 43 Hurricanes arrived safely at Alexandria. The arrival of fifteen long-range Beaufighters at Malta permitted an 'umbrella' for the passage through the narrows, while *Formidable*'s fighters kept off assailants that were able to find the convoy during the fine spells. Tragically the poor visibility which prevailed for so much of the time was responsible for the loss of many of *Formidable*'s fighters, a feature which was to be irremediable before the battle for Crete. As she steamed into Alexandria once again, on May 12th, just two months after her arrival in the Mediterranean, during which she had covered thousands of miles and seen much action, she was down to her last four Fulmar fighters.

On the arrival of the British in Crete in 1940 there were no airfields sufficiently developed for operational use, but there was a landing ground near Heraklion which could be used for refuelling British aircraft flying between Egypt and Greece. This was enlarged, and another site to the south-eastward was prepared by the RAF to permit the landing of bombers. These two airfields near Heraklion were however fifty miles eastward of Suda Bay, too far to operate efficient fighter protection for that base. It was for this reason that the site at Maleme, eight miles to the westward of Canea and Suda, was taken over for development by the Fleet Air Arm.

It is important to realise the difficulties and the shortages which beset attempts to develop an effective defence in Crete, owing to the primitive nature of the island and lack of communication. There were no railways, and only one good road full of hairpin bends which ran along the northern coast; south of this was the mountainous volcanic range running like a backbone throughout the whole length of 150 miles, and rising in places to 8,000 feet. Apart from the fine harbour at Suda Bay, sheltered from the north by the Akrotiri peninsula, there were two other ports on the north coast; Heraklion which could take a destroyer, and Retimo which could accept only small coasters. On the south coast, about twenty miles from Suda Bay as the crow flies, was the fishing village of Sphakia, but the rough road leading towards it stopped abruptly in the mountains several miles short of the village.

After the British occupation of Crete in October 1940, Suda Bay had become an important fuelling base for Cunningham's light forces, especially for destroyers, enabling them to operate for longer periods in the Aegean Sea and in the central Mediterranean. Of the 21,000 British and Imperial troops evacuated from Greece in April, and taken to Crete, most were without equipment except for rifles. They were organised for the defence of the island and placed under the command of Freyberg on April 30th. These troops, together with the original British garrison, and last minute British reinforcements from the Middle East command, brought the total strength to some 32,000, and included 6,500 Australians and 7,000 New Zealanders, supplemented by a number of young Greek troops short of arms but making up in spirit what they lacked in experience. A few old tanks were also sent in, but there appeared to be some reluctance in relinquishing from the Cyrenaica front, any of the recently arrived 238 tanks brought to Alexandria in the Tiger convoy. In the event, the old tanks proved unreliable and hazardous owing to breakdowns.

It is of interest to record that a widespread feeling prevailed at that time among service personnel, that having been kicked out of Greece, mainly because of enemy superiority in the air, it could not be long before British and Imperial forces were driven out of Crete. There was a hopeless shortage, not of men, but of the wherewithal of war: tanks, anti-aircraft guns, transport, and communications equipment. The official view was that Crete must be held, and would be held, provided the coming assault came only from the air, which must necessarily limit the number of enemy troops which could be landed safely to only a few thousand.

Freyberg divided the island for purposes of defence into two main areas: Maleme to Retimo, with his headquarters at Canea; and Heraklion as a separate and detached command to the eastward, with the original British garrison of the island under Brigadier B. H. Chappel. His own area he divided into three sections: Maleme to Suda, to be held by New Zealand troops under Brigadier E. Puttick; Suda to be held by British troops under Major-General E. C. Weston, RM; Georgiopolis to Retimo to be held by Australian troops under Brigadier G. A. Vasey.

Facilities for unloading the British supply ships which arrived at Suda Bay were limited, and were subjected to ever-increasing bombing attacks during daylight hours. Between April 30th and May 20th, fifteen supply ships arrived, of which eight were sunk or damaged while in harbour. It was possible to get only 15,000 tons of stores ashore during this time.

Meanwhile, elsewhere the Germans, with great speed and exertion, and practically unmolested, were enlarging old airfields and constructing new ones in forward areas (miles from Suda shown in brackets) such as: Milos (75), Molaci (100), Scarpanto (150). Here they concentrated their dive bombers and single-engined fighters. Twin-engined fighters were assembled in the Athens area only 200 miles away. The operation for the airborne assault in Crete was originated by General Student, and was to be carried out by some 13,000 parachute and airborne troops with 700 bombers and fighters (of which 50 were allocated to reconnaissance), 530 transport aircraft, 72 gliders.

Hitler had agreed to the operation only after assurance from Goering that it could be conducted entirely by air and completed in a few days. Hitler was already preparing for his drive into Russia and was concerned at the threat to the Ploesti oilfields posed by the British retention of Crete, but was reassured by Goering that the planned role for the Luftwaffe in the Russian campaign would not be delayed. The assault was scheduled for May 17th but delayed until May 20th because 2,500,000 gallons of aircraft fuel had to be brought by sea down the Adriatic coast from Trieste.

As already mentioned, the plan was that Maleme was to be taken on the forenoon of the first day, and Retimo and Heraklion the same afternoon. By 05.00 hrs on May 20th the first of the transports were airborne, and the troops now had time to read some of the instructions which had been handed to them:

'You are the chosen ones of the German army . . . To you the battle shall be fulfilment.'

'Beware of talking.'
'Be calm, prudent, strong, and resolute.'
'Never surrender.'

Already on this beautiful sunny morning, the air above Crete was thick with smoke from the preliminary bombing phase.

CHAPTER THREE

British Naval Operational Plan Before the German Assault

Back at Alexandria on May 12th, on completion of Tiger convoy (a 'memorable achievement' according to the Admiralty), Cunningham received intelligence that the air assault on Crete could be expected as early as May 15th. This would mean little respite for the fleet, and permitted small chance of rest and replenishment of fuel and ammunition. Nevertheless by May 15th Vice-Admiral H. D. Pridham-Wippell, CVO, was on station to the west of Crete with a powerful Force A.

Cunningham had given much consideration to naval requirements which must be able to prevent enemy seaborne landings regardless of enemy air superiority, and at the same time be ready to meet any sortie by the Italian fleet. Hitherto he had flown his flag at sea in the battleship *Warspite* in company with the battle fleet and an aircraft carrier (now the *Formidable*), while Pridham-Wippell as Vice-Admiral Light Forces had flown his flag in the cruiser *Orion*: this had been the organisation at the battle of Matapan. Now however Cunningham decided to station four different forces in order to carry out nightly sweeps in the enemy approaches to Crete, withdrawing from dangerous areas at night. The reader will be better able to understand the complexity of subsequent events, and the spontaneous intermixing of the four forces during developments, by a careful inspection of diagram 2 showing the respective areas to be swept. In a position well to the westward of Crete was to be Force A consisting of two battleships and five destroyers to cover the possible appearance of heavy units of the Italian fleet. Farther north, sweeping an area between Cape Matapan and Sapienza Island, Force B (two cruisers) would cover the north-western approaches. Sweeping the area Antikithera to Piraeus was Force D, with responsibility to prevent any landings west of Retimo. Force D (two cruisers and two destroyers) would be supported by Force B if necessary. To the eastward in the area Kaso to Leros, Force C was to sweep and deal with landings at Heraklion and Sitia (see diag. 1).

With four dispersed forces at sea Cunningham considered it imperative to direct the naval side of operations from his HQ at Alexandria, where positions of all ships could be plotted hour by hour on a large-scale chart in the war room close to his office, and from which communications would be unhampered. Air reconnaissance was arranged but this was thin and would remain so while the *Formidable* was compelled to stay in harbour for want of adequate fighter strength.

The most probable landing places for a seaborne assault were thought to be Canea, Retimo, and Heraklion. There were also possibilities, though less likely, at the western and eastern extremities of the island, at Kissamo and Sitia.

In addition to preventing German seaborne landings, the navy had to provide for reinforcements and supplies to the British and Imperial troops ashore in Crete. A battalion of the Leinster Regiment with full equipment was landed at night on May 15th at Heraklion by the cruisers *Gloucester* and *Fiji*. Two nights later, the special service ship *Glengyle* landed 700 men of the Argyll and Sutherland Highlanders at Tymbaki, an anchorage on the south coast of Crete, 25 miles over the mountains from Heraklion. Three I tanks (infantry) were also landed from Tank Landing Craft No 2.

Farther afield from the areas allocated to Forces A, B, C, and D, there were to be minefields, one laid by the fast minelayer *Abdiel* between Cephalonia and Levkos, to interrupt enemy passage through the Corinth Canal, the other laid by the minelaying submarine *Rorqual* in the vicinity of Lemnos. An inshore squadron of five MTBs based on Suda was to supervise coastal traffic.

On the evening of May 14th both Force A and Force D sailed in company from Alexandria for Cretan waters. Cunningham was a great believer in concentration of fire-power, particularly so for his ships' anti-aircraft guns. His continuing aggressive approach was based on the opinion that it took exceptional air strength to neutralise efficient warships when manoeuvred at high speed by experienced captains. Force A comprised the two battleships *Queen Elizabeth* (flagship of Pridham-Wippell) and *Barham*, with five destroyers

Diagram 2. (*Opposite*) The Eastern Mediterranean.

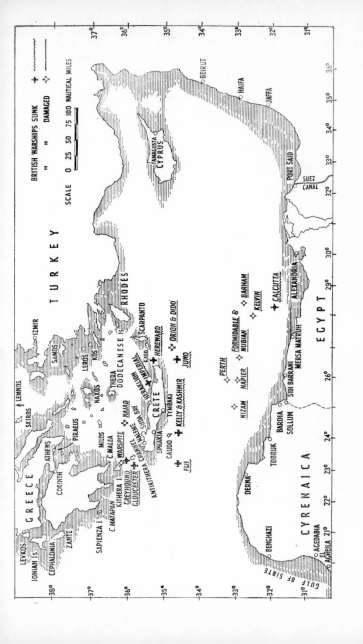

Jervis, Jaguar, Nizam, Defender, and *Imperial.*★   Force D consisted of the two light cruisers *Naiad* and *Phoebe,* with two destroyers *Greyhound* and *Hasty,* under the command of Rear-Admiral E. L. S. King, CB, MVO, flying his flag in the *Naiad.*   The *Phoebe* however developed a defect compelling her immediate return to Alexandria, and her place in Force D was taken by HMAS *Perth.*

Cover was provided by this combination of Forces A and D for a convoy on passage from Alexandria to Crete on May 15th.   The Forces then proceeded together in preparation to begin their allocated tasks, and were joined on May 16th by Force B consisting of the two heavy cruisers *Gloucester* and *Fiji,* and the destroyers *Hotspur* and *Havock.*   The latter Force had landed reinforcements at Suda the previous night.   The destroyer *Ilex* also joined early on May 16th, and throughout the day all ten destroyers refuelled, taking 1,289 tons of oil from the two battleships.

There was still no news of any assault, and only the intensified bombing of Crete could indicate that the attack might not long be delayed.   Meanwhile Force C comprising the light cruiser *Dido* and the old anti-aircraft light cruiser *Coventry* together with destroyers *Juno, Kandahar, Kingston,* and *Nubian,* under the command of Rear-Admiral I. G. Glennie (flag in *Dido*) proceeded towards the southward of the dangerous Kaso Strait: dangerous because of its close proximity to newly-supplied German airfields in the island of Scarpanto.   And following the refuelling of destroyers on May 16th Forces B and D proceeded in readiness to take up their pre-arranged sweeps.   In the light of the intelligence available, however, there appeared to be no enemy convoys on passage, and it was therefore not yet deemed expedient for either Force D or Force C to enter the Aegean.

On the following day, May 17th, it was decided to relieve the covering Force A by ships which had been kept in reserve at Alexandria.   A reserve Force A1 therefore sailed on May 18th from Alexandria after dark, comprising the two battleships *Warspite* and *Valiant,* the light cruiser *Ajax,* and eight destroyers, *Napier, Kimberley, Janus, Isis, Hereward, Decoy, Hero,* and *Griffin,* under the command of Rear-Admiral H. B. Rawlings, OBE, flying his flag in the *Warspite.* The relief took place on May 19th to the south-west of Crete, and Pridham-Wippell returned with the ships of the original Force A to Alexandria, excepting *Imperial* which together with the *Hotspur* was assigned to Force A1 under Rawlings' command.   Forces B, C, and

★ For technical particulars see Appendix B

D also sailed for Alexandria to refuel, and on completion returned to Crete to resume their individual roles of patrol, but with King now assuming with his force the role of Force C; and Glennie that of Force D.

This all sounds fairly straightforward, but the reader need not stretch the imagination very far to realise the immense amount of signalling required to pass each Commander's instructions and counter-instructions concerning night intentions during the constant expectation of the enemy assault and the continued preparedness necessary to squash any seaborne expedition. During this phase *Greyhound* (Commander W. R. Marshall-A'Deane, DSO, DSC) passed to King, the commander of Force D, 'The road to Crete is paved with Night Intentions'.

Since refuelling led to a regrouping, it is necessary to indicate the new composition of these groups, which by daylight on May 20th, on the morning of the German airborne assault on Crete, was as follows:

Force A1: *Warspite*, *Valiant*, and five destroyers *Napier*, *Hereward*, *Decoy*, *Hero*, *Hotspur* under Rawlings, 100 miles west of Crete.
Force B: *Gloucester*, *Fiji*, and two destroyers *Greyhound* and *Griffin* under Captain Rowley, on passage to rendezvous with Rawlings.
Force C: *Naiad*, *Perth*, and four destroyers *Kandahar*, *Kingston*, *Nubian*, and *Juno* under King, southward of the Kaso Strait.
Force D: *Dido*, *Orion*, *Ajax*, and four destroyers *Isis*, *Kimberley*, *Imperial*, and *Janus* under Glennie, west of the Antikithera Channel.

It was during the preliminary phase on May 18th that the first Victoria Cross to be awarded to the Mediterranean Fleet during the war was won by Petty Officer A. E. Sephton, the director gunlayer of the anti-aircraft cruiser *Coventry* of Force C. South of Crete the *Coventry* had gone to the assistance of the hospital ship ABA which was being attacked by seven Ju87s. The latter then transferred their attack to the *Coventry*, raking her with machine-gun fire, and a bullet passed through Sephton's back. Though in great pain Sephton refused help and continued to direct the fire until the attackers were driven off. He died the next day. His action may well have saved both the *Coventry* and the ABA.

CHAPTER FOUR

Sea Power Against Air Power

WEDNESDAY MAY 21ST

As soon as he heard that the air assault on Crete had begun, on Tuesday May 20th, Cunningham ordered those forces that were at sea to close Crete, but to keep out of sight of land during daylight. The main search areas of the respective forces as delineated in Chapter Three were to remain much the same, but it should be appreciated that the constitution of forces especially in the matter of destroyers would vary because of the constant need to miss no opportunity for refuelling.★ Over and above the requirements for both strategic and tactical moves, therefore, there had to be unremitting consideration for expenditure of ammunition and fuel, factors which were to prove crucial in the battle of ships against aircraft.

Orders for the night were that Force B, consisting of the heavy cruisers *Gloucester* and *Fiji* and two destroyers, should pass close to Cape Matapan at 04.00hrs on the Wednesday, and then rendezvous with the heavy covering Force A1 at 07.00hrs, fifty miles west of Crete. A British aircraft report of caiques in the Aegean Sea caused Cunningham to amend instructions to Force C and Force D who were now ordered to establish patrols in the northern approaches to Crete: Force C under King to the east of the meridian of 25° East; Force D under Glennie to the west of that longitude.

While approaching the Kaso Strait at 20.40hrs on Tuesday May 20th shortly after sunset, Force C was attacked by torpedo-carrying aircraft; all torpedoes were avoided. An hour later six enemy motor boats were encountered in the dark, and were engaged by the destroyers *Juno*, *Kandahar*, and the cruiser *Naiad*, whereupon the boats retired, four of them damaged.

The position ashore at the end of Tuesday the first day of the assault was regarded by General Student as critical; the stiffness of the opposition had come as an unpleasant surprise, and Student had

★ See Appendix J—Destroyer Endurance Range

achieved only a fraction of what he had set out to do. He subsequently wrote:

'If the enemy had made a united all-out effort in counter-attacking that night, . . . or in the morning of the 21st, then the very tired remnants of the Sturm Regiments, suffering from lack of ammunition, could have been wiped out.'

The situation from Freyberg's point of view was not unsatisfactory, although it was impossible to get an accurate picture. About 2,000 troops had been dropped at Maleme, and the invader's losses had been severe. The airfield had not been captured, although the western fringe was in German hands. Of the 6,000 troops dropped at Canea, Retimo, and Heraklion, roughly half had been killed or captured. Freyberg was still much concerned about the possibility of a sea-borne attack, and was reluctant to move troops or weaken certain strategic points. Nothing further however was sighted at sea that night.

In accordance with previous orders a new Force E comprising the destroyers *Jervis*, *Nizam*, and *Ilex*, under the command of Captain P. J. Mack, DSO, proceeded during the night to the Italian island of Scarpanto, fifty miles east of Crete, and at 02.45hrs on Wednesday May 21st bombarded the airfield. Darkness precluded observation of results, but it was later learned that two D17 aircraft were damaged. Following the bombardment Force E proceeded to Pegadia Bay on the east coast of Scarpanto, six miles north of the airfield, and finding no enemy forces there, retired to the southward, being later recalled to Alexandria.

Following its night sweep into the Aegean which had produced nothing more than an encounter with motor boats, King's Force C withdrew through the Kaso Strait just before sunrise on Wednesday May 21st, being joined then by the *Calcutta* and that afternoon by the *Carlisle*. Both of these anti-aircraft cruisers were fresh from Alexandria. King's Force C suffered several aircraft attacks from daylight onwards as he proceeded southwards from the Kaso Strait, being bombed almost continuously for the four hours between 09.50hrs and 13.50hrs either by Italian high level bombers or by German dive bombers, all of whom revelled in the absence of fighter opposition. Great havoc was performed however by the guns of the cruisers *Naiad*, *Perth*, *Calcutta*, *Carlisle*, and the destroyers *Kandahar*, *Kingston*, *Nubian*, and *Juno*, inflicting casualties which included at least one aircraft shot down and two damaged. At 12.49hrs the *Juno* was hit by a bomb during an Italian high level attack, which penetrated her magazine and exploded. She sank in two minutes. Six officers and 91 ratings were picked up by the destroyers. But there was great loss of life, including the First Lieutenant Walter Starkie, a fellow staff officer of the writer, at Dartmouth just before the outbreak of the war, an officer highly regarded in the service, who had relinquished his job as Flag Lieutenant to the Commander-in-Chief for a more active life in destroyers. His widow was Cunningham's niece. A petty officer Edwin Lumley, blown over the side and badly burned, swam 40 yards in a thick layer of floating oil fuel to rescue a shipmate in difficulties.

In the meantime during this day Wednesday May 21st the other forces were having a relatively quiet time with less attention from the air than that suffered by King's Force C, and every opportunity was taken between air attacks for destroyers to refuel from the battleships. At daylight Glennie's Force D had been northward of Canea Bay, and having sighted nothing during the night was with-drawing westward towards the Antikithera Channel to close Rawlings's heavy covering Force A1 which lay sixty miles to the west of the Channel. At the same time Force A1 was being closed by Force B which had had an uneventful night sweep between Cape Matapan and Cape Elophonesi at the south-west point of Crete.

It is clear that the enemy's greatest concern on this day, Wednesday May 21st, was to improve their position at Maleme and Canea with the reckless determination to saturate the airfield with airborne troops sent in every five minutes, regardless of the opposition. Bombing and fighter strafing of defence positions continued unabated.

The size of the formidable naval forces remaining during that day to the south-west of Kithera, refuelling and awaiting reports of enemy convoys that might be at sea, can be gathered from the following list:

Force A1: The battleships *Warspite* and *Valiant*, and the destroyers *Napier*, *Decoy*, *Hero*, and *Hotspur* under Rawlings.
Force B: The heavy cruisers *Gloucester* and *Fiji*, and the destroyers *Griffin* and *Greyhound* under Rowley.
Force D: The light cruisers *Dido*, *Orion*, *Ajax*, and the destroyers *Janus*, *Kimberley*, *Hasty*, and *Hereward* under Glennie

With the concentration of such a large force it was possible to put up an anti-aircraft barrage over the fleet which effectively reduced the severity of the dive bombing attacks and inflicted casualties, probably two aircraft being shot down. The *Ajax* suffered damage from a near miss which affected her speed, but the damage was rectified before nightfall. All seemed well while the ammunition lasted, but the expenditure during daylight hours was enormous, and the vulnerability of this large force which including Force C consisted of two battleships, nine cruisers, and thirteen destroyers, increased hourly as the attacks continued. The fast minelayer *Abdiel* had returned this day to Alexandria after laying mines off Cephalonia in a position adjacent to Force B's area of sweep.

During the afternoon of Wednesday May 21st a Maryland of the RAF No 39 Squadron reported groups of small craft escorted by warships proceeding southward from the island of Milos towards Crete, in a position about eighty miles north of Retimo. Here at last were the enemy seaborne landing troops. Glennie's Force D was to go in at dusk, while Rowley's Force B stood guard in the Antikithera Strait to prevent any Italian naval forces breaking in from the west. Rawlings's Force A1 was to be in a strategic position to the south-west ready to give support as required, and in fact followed Force D well into the Antikithera Strait to provide anti-aircraft gun support until sunset, after which it turned westward to take up patrol duty in the support area. As the two forces parted company Force D was subjected to an attack by four Ju88s of which three were shot down. Glennie wrote in his report:

'A pleasing start to the night's operations.'

Meanwhile King's Force C was to re-enter through the Kaso Strait and resume patrol of the eastern section during the night in search of enemy seaborne forces. Also on this Wednesday evening the 5th Destroyer Flotilla consisting of the *Kelly*, *Kashmir*, *Kipling*, *Kelvin*, and *Jackal*, under the command of Captain Lord Louis Mountbatten, GCVO, DSO, proceeded from Malta to join Rawlings's depleted Force A1 the next morning.

Aided by radar, Glennie's Force D encountered the reported enemy troop convoy at 23.30 hrs on Wednesday May 21st, when eighteen miles north of Canea. The convoy comprised a score or so of caiques and small Greek cargo ships loaded with German troops to the number of more than a thousand (first reports said 4,000) and heavy equipment in the form of transport vehicles, guns, and tanks, destined for Suda Bay, and headed by the Italian destroyer *Lupo* (Commander Francesco Mimbelli). This desperate measure with scant naval support had been decided upon following the serious setback received by the German air assault on the first day. When within a few miles of Canea the convoy was taken completely by surprise, the gallant little *Lupo* at once laid a smoke screen for the protection of the convoy and went into the attack firing torpedoes and guns. There was great confusion in the dark as the British destroyers hurled themselves on the caiques, sinking them by ramming and by gunfire in a mêlée which lasted for more than two hours. More than half were sunk, and a thousand troops were killed or thrown into the sea. An Italian report* by Commander Bragadin says:

> 'Under a hail of shells falling on his ship, Commander Mimbelli directed the *Lupo* through the British formation between the *Ajax* and *Orion*, came close aboard a cruiser (*Dido*), and passed just a few metres from its stern, all the while exchanging heavy gun and machine gun fire ... While these shells killed and wounded many men, they caused no mortal damage to the ship, which made good her escape despite the *Ajax*'s claim that it had "pulverised" the Italian vessel.'

Glennie called off his scattered force at 03.30hrs on Thursday May 22nd in view of the general shortage of ammunition. His flagship the *Dido* had only 30 per cent remaining, and the *Orion* and *Ajax* were down to 38 per cent and 42 per cent respectively, and he felt little justified in carrying out the previously planned sweep to the northward at daylight. Instead he turned to the westward to proceed to a rendezvous for his scattered ships thirty miles west of Crete, and with the intention of joining Rawlings's Force A1. By 09.30hrs on Thursday May 22nd, however, *Dido*'s anti-aircraft ammunition was down to 25 per cent, and that of the *Orion* and the *Ajax* 38 per cent and 40 per cent respectively with the prospect of a heavy day of air attacks ahead. Cunningham ordered Glennie's force to return to Alexandria with all despatch. While endorsing Glennie's opinion that the *Dido* was in no condition to comply with orders to sweep northward, Cunningham later considered that the *Ajax* and the *Orion* should have remained to assist other forces as they were compara-

* 'The Italian Navy in WWII'. USNI Annapolis 1957

Above: C-in-C of the Mediterranean Fleet, Admiral Sir Andrew Brown Cunningham, KCB, DSO (later Admiral of the Fleet Viscount Cunningham of Hyndhope, KT, GCB, OM, DSO)

Below left: Second-in-Command Mediterranean Fleet, Vice-Admiral Sir Henry Pridham-Wippell, KCB, CVO

Below right: Commander Defence Forces, Crete, Major-General B. C. Freyberg, VC, CB, CMG, DSO

Left: Originator of the airborne assault, and commander of Fliegerkorps XI, General Kurt Student

Below: In overall command, Colonel-General Alexander Lohr (right) with Luftwaffe officer

Above left: Vice-Admiral E. L. S. King, CB, MVO

Above right: Vice-Admiral Sir Henry B. Rawlings, KCB, OBE

Below: Rear-Admiral I. G. Glennie

Luftwaffe Colonel Brauer with paratroop lieutenant

Captain Lord Louis Mountbatten, GCVO, DSO, of the 5th Destroyer Flotilla

Top: A Ju52 German transport plane

Above: A Ju87B German dive-bomber

Top: The German air attack on Suda Bay

Above: German parachutes descending from their transport planes. The parachute clusters of four carry trucks, field guns, and motor vehicles

A crashed German glider

The retreating rearguard undertook some demolition work

HMS *Queen Elizabeth*

HMS *Barham* (damaged May 27th, 1941)

HMS *Warspite* (severely damaged May 22nd, 1941)

HMS *Valiant* in which Prince Philip was serving

Top: HMS *Formidable*, which was hit twice and severely damaged on May 26th, 1941

Above: A near miss, one of many seen from the *Formidable* before finally being put out of action for several months on May 26th, 1941   [*Formidable*

HMS *Gloucester* (sunk May 22nd, 1941) [*The Times*

HMS *Fiji* (sunk May 22nd, 1941)

HMAS *Perth*, HMS *Ajax*, and HMS *Orion* steaming westward
on the morning of Matapan, March 28th, 1941; all were
seriously damaged at Crete two months later
[Canberra Australian War Memorial

HMAS *Perth* (badly damaged May 22nd, and May 30th, 1941)

Top: HMS *Ajax* of River Plate and Matapan fame, which was damaged on May 21st, and May 28th, 1941

Above: HMS *Orion* (severely damaged May 29th, 1941)

HMS *Dido* (severely damaged May 29th, 1941)

HMS *Phoebe*, which completed two Crete evacuation trips

HMS *Naiad* (damaged May 22nd, 1941)

The fast mine-layer HMS *Abdiel*

The anti-aircraft cruiser HMS *Carlisle*, which was damaged on May 22nd, 1941

HMS *Calcutta* in 1919 (sunk June 1st, 1941)

tively well off for ammunition. In the light of the situation in the Aegean on Thursday forenoon the presence of these two ships would have been invaluable. Glennie could not however have foreseen that, and was by then already on his way to Alexandria for replenishment.

It was during the night of Wednesday May 21st and the morning of Thursday May 22nd that Freyberg's counter-attack to take Maleme airfield was mounted. It was intended to take also the higher ground overlooking the airfield. The 5th New Zealand Brigade were to be committed, beginning with a night march to concentration points and developing into a full assault just before dawn. Unfortunately it was intended that their move forward was to take place only after relief in their existing positions by an Australian battalion which in the event was seriously delayed by a number of misfortunes. The carefully planned counter-attack, limited in scope already by the continuing necessity to provide against possible seaborne attack, appeared to be destined for failure; a failure in spite of determined hand-to-hand fighting with bayonet and grenade by the gallant New Zealanders just before dawn. Almost all the ground lost had been recaptured by dawn, but the airfield itself remained in German hands, and from dawn onwards big Ju52s arrived at the rate of almost one a minute, each transport plane depositing forty fully equipped men.

Meanwhile Cunningham had ordered Force B, *Gloucester*, *Fiji*, *Griffin*, and *Greyhound*, to break off their patrol off Cape Matapan and to proceed with despatch into the Aegean to Heraklion where the harbour was reported to be in enemy hands. No enemy was sighted but Rowley's force was continuously dive-bombed from sunrise onwards until at 08.30hrs on this Thursday forenoon he had rejoined Rawlings's Force A1 well west of Kithera. Slight damage was sustained by each cruiser. But so far, apart from the lucky hit on *Juno*, the fleet had survived remarkably well in spite of local enemy air superiority. The wear and tear and fatigue had been enormous, and the expenditure of ammunition was on a scale that could not be maintained indefinitely.

CHAPTER FIVE

Darkest Hour

THURSDAY MAY 22ND

Thursday May 22nd was to be a particularly sad day for Cunningham's fleet. Positions at daylight were as follows. Rawlings with his Force A1 was about forty-five miles south-west of Kithera, proceeding to the north-westward, shortly to be joined during the forenoon by Rowley's Force B after his sweep into the Aegean, and Mountbatten who had sailed from Malta with his five destroyers of the 5th Destroyer Flotilla the previous evening. King's Force C was in the Aegean off Heraklion beginning a sweep to the north-westward in search of any further enemy troop convoys that might be approaching Crete. Force D would shortly be on its way to Alexandria for replenishment. Coming from Alexandria were Captain H. M. L. Waller, DSO, RAN, of the 10th Destroyer Flotilla, with the *Stuart, Voyager,* and *Vendetta,* which were to reinforce Rawlings's Force A1, and Captain P. J. Mack, DSO, of the 14th Destroyer Flotilla, with the *Jervis, Nizam,* and *Ilex,* the Force E (minus the *Decoy*) which had bombarded Scarpanto. Mack's destroyers were to give support to King's Force C (four cruisers *Naiad, Perth, Calcutta, Carlisle,* three destroyers *Kandahar, Kingston,* and *Nubian*). King was to need all the support possible for his daylight sweep to the north-westward from Heraklion, a perilous but essential task if enemy seaborne attempts were to be frustrated. The army defenders would have enough to worry about from airborne assaults alone.

Nothing had been sighted during the night. Air attacks on King's ships began at 07.00hrs and continued incessantly on this Thursday forenoon. After an hour and a half of continuous attacks from the air, Force C sighted a single caique carrying German troops. King's position at this time 08.30hrs, well known to enemy bombers, was some thirty miles north of Retimo and about sixty miles south of Milos, one of the German advanced bombing bases. Every minute took his force closer. Every attack resulted in further massive expenditure of ammunition. The caique was sunk by the *Perth* which, being under heavy air attack herself at that moment, was joined by the *Naiad* to give anti-aircraft support. In view of the need for wide reconnaissance King's ships would have to be spread, a factor inconsistent with the close concentration required for an intense barrage against attacking aircraft. At 09.09hrs the *Calcutta* reported a small merchant vessel, and destroyers were sent in to deal with her. An hour later at 10.10hrs an Italian destroyer (the *Sagittario*) was reported together with five small sailing vessels. By this time Force C was only twenty-five miles south of Milos. The *Perth* had rejoined the rest of the force, but the *Naiad* was labouring some distance astern, under very heavy air attack. The whole force engaged the *Sagittario* which retired behind smoke after firing torpedoes. The *Kingston* claimed hits at a range of 7,000 yards, and reported a large number of caiques behind the smoke. The convoy consisted of 38 caiques carrying 4,000 troops to be landed at Heraklion, together with small steamships loaded with guns and tanks. The convoy had already been recalled by the German Admiral Schuster as a result of Glennie's action in the early hours of Thursday May 22nd, though it is uncertain whether this order had been received before the sudden encounter with Admiral King's force.

Though King was not to know about that, he now had to make a crucial decision. So far his ships had escaped with minor damage but speed was now limited to 21 knots owing to the *Carlisle* being unable to steam any faster. They were running short of ammunition and had to be kept together for mutual support. Would he be justified in jeopardising perhaps the whole of his force by proceeding farther to the northward? Even now they were seventy or eighty miles from the Kithera Strait to reach which would require at least four more hours of steaming under heavy attack. He made his decision, recalled the destroyers from the chase and proceeded westward. A signal from Cunningham made at 09.41hrs indicating that the enemy convoy was of considerable size was not seen by King until 11.00hrs, by which time he was well committed to the westward and under continuous air attack. Cunningham considered King's decision a faulty one, and believed that the destruction of this large convoy would have justified severe losses. With characteristic comment he stated that the safest place for King's force was among the ships of the enemy convoy. This may appear to be sound, but it assumes a degree of recognition and discrimination among the enemy bombers not borne out in operations.

Bragadin* says of this action:

'At 08.30hrs on May 22nd destroyer escort *Sagittario* (Lieutenant Fulgosi)) . . . received orders to return to Milos because of the precarious ground situation. . . . As soon as the British group of cruisers and destroyers under Admiral King sighted the *Sagittario* [and the 30 small vessels], they came on to meet it opening fire from 12,000 metres. The enemy shells were landing all around . . . but by zigzagging rapidly the *Sagittario* succeeded in avoiding the concentrated fire of the seven opposing ships. When less than 8,000 metres away from the second cruiser, Fulgosi headed straight at it and launched his torpedoes. . . . However the British ships ceased firing and pulled away to the south-west.'

Probably no one was more surprised than Fulgosi, who was now 'attacked by several Stukas five times'. But his gallant little ship was unharmed, and under cover of his smoke screen much of the large convoy had escaped.

During his withdrawal to the westward King was bombed continuously for $3\frac{1}{2}$ hours. It seemed that on this day, Thursday, there was overwhelming enemy air strength over the ships, perhaps because the bombers were less preoccupied with the bombing of land targets. The light cruiser *Naiad* had two turrets put out of action, and near misses caused several of her compartments to be flooded and her speed to be reduced to 17 or 18 knots. In the course of ten minutes there were 36 misses, and during a period of two hours 181 bombs were counted. Only two of her turrets remained in action. At 11.25hrs, as he was unable to keep up with the remainder of his force King ordered the ships back to his support. The *Carlisle* was now hit, though with little resulting damage, and the *Perth* had her armament control put out of action.

Meanwhile Rawlings with Force A1 and Force B had been patrolling twenty to thirty miles westward of the Kithera Channel, 'serving a useful purpose' as he put it, 'by attracting enemy aircraft'. Ships always found it consoling when under heavy air attack to see that there were other ships to share the load. As soon as he heard that King would be withdrawing from the Aegean, Rawlings decided to meet him in the neighbourhood of the Kithera Channel. At 12.25hrs,

* 'The Italian Navy in WW II'. USNI. Annapolis 1957

upon hearing further of the *Naiad*'s reduced speed and Force C's need for support, Rawlings steered for the Channel at his maximum speed of 23 knots, with the intention of entering the Aegean. This must have been a difficult decision involving as it did the great vulnerability of his two battleships, whose 15in guns would be useless against attacking aircraft. Their reserve of anti-aircraft amunition was however good, being 66 per cent in the *Warspite* and 80 per cent in the *Valiant*. Those in the cruisers of Force B on the other hand were dangerously low, being only 18 per cent remaining in the *Gloucester* and 30 per cent in the *Fiji*.

As King's sorely pressed Force C approached the Channel, a Messerschmitt dived at the *Carlisle* spraying the bridge with machine-gun fire, and killing her commanding officer Captain T. C. Hampton. A few minutes later, at 13.12hrs, King's anti-aircraft shell bursts were sighted by Rawlings, and twenty minutes later still the Forces C, A1, and B joined and withdrew together to the south-westward. At this very moment, 13.32hrs, the *Warspite* was dive-bombed by three Messerschmitts. Emerging suddenly from low cloud they attacked her with great determination end-on, down the fore and aft line. One of the released bombs hit her on the starboard side, wrecking her 4in and 6in batteries. Her boiler room fan intakes were also damaged, and her speed thereby reduced to 18 knots. Shortly before this a large caique had been sighted between the islands of Pori and Antikithera, and the destroyer *Greyhound* was ordered to sink her. Rear-Admiral King being senior to Rear-Admiral Rawlings now assumed command of the combined forces.

In spite of the concentrated and incessant bombing attacks around Crete, skilful manoeuvre together with lively anti-aircraft fire from the ships of the fleet had so far resulted in little loss and relatively small damage. The situation was now to take a drastic turn on this calamitous day. The first casualty was the destroyer *Greyhound*, the little ship that had revealed with her searchlight the large force of Italian ships on the night of the action off Matapan, less than a month earlier. Having sunk the caique in accordance with instructions, she was returning to resume her place in Force A1's destroyer screen when at 13.51hrs she was attacked by eight dive bombers and struck by two bombs; another example of a ship's vulnerability when separated from the main body. She sank in fifteen minutes, her guns firing to the last, and having launched a whaler, the only sound boat left.

King at once detached the destroyers *Kandahar* and *Kingston* to pick up survivors, and shortly after 14.00hrs, because of the almost continuous bombing and machine-gun attacks on the rescue operations, ordered the heavy cruisers *Gloucester* and *Fiji* to stand by the rescuing destroyers and give anti-aircraft support, while the remainder of the fleet retired south-westward. At this stage he was unaware of the sadly depleted stocks of ammunition in Force B.

Supported by the cruisers, the *Kandahar* and *Kingston* lowered boats and picked up a number of survivors from the *Greyhound* including her commanding officer Commander W. R. Marshall-A'Deane, DSO, DSC. Cunningham in *A Sailor's Odyssey*, refers to a visit some days later to the wounded in hospital at Alexandria. He was told by a young ordinary seaman who had got away in the *Greyhound*'s whaler with about twenty survivors that upon seeing an enemy aircraft coming straight at them he had dived overboard and swum underwater. On surfacing he looked into the boat to find every man dead from machine-gunning. These included the first lieutenant Lieutenant Robin Scott (whom the writer had taught at Dartmouth in 1929), the engineer officer Lieutenant-Commander (E) R. E. G. Bremner, and Mr J. W. Chase the Warrant Gunner (T): all unarmed and defenceless.

The rescuing ships were taking such a pasting that at 14.56hrs King, now aware of depleted ammunition stocks, ordered the ships to withdraw after dropping boats and rafts, and then to join him. There had been no hits on the ships, but the *Kingston* had been damaged by three near misses.

By 15.30hrs the *Gloucester* and *Fiji* were seen to be coming up at high speed astern of the main force. Twenty minutes later, the gallant *Gloucester* which had survived so many bomb attacks in the past was seen to receive several hits. She was brought to a standstill enveloped in raging fires, her upper deck a shambles. She could not possibly last much longer. The *Fiji* closed to drop floats and boats, but in view of the intensity of air attacks and the depleted stocks of ammunition and oil fuel her captain reluctantly decided that the *Fiji*, together with the destroyers *Kandahar* and *Kingston*, must withdraw to the southward. They were hotly pursued by aircraft. As they proceeded they were cheered by the swimming *Gloucester* survivors now awaiting machine-gunning from the air. It was hoped that some might reach land, not far distant, but loss of life was high and included Captain H. A. Rowley. Also lost were the first lieutenant Lieutenant-Commander John Brett, and Captain Dick Formby, RM, two most promising officers who had been on the staff of the RN College at Dartmouth with the writer at the outbreak of the war. 'Gloucester' was an old and particularly loved name in the Royal Navy. An earlier distinguished holder of the name had been one of the ships connected with Anson's famous voyage round the world 1740–1744.

Steaming southward at 27 knots with the two destroyers, the *Fiji* successfully fought off no less than twenty bombing attacks in the next four hours, but this isolated little force was steadily drawing farther away from the fleet. At 17.10hrs *Fiji* had reported her position as twenty-four miles 305° from Cape Elophonesi, the south-west corner of Crete, which placed her as being thirty miles due east of Forces C and A1, who were at that time steaming 215°. But at 18.45hrs her luck forsook her when she fell a victim to a single Messerschmitt coming out of the clouds in a shallow dive. With a near miss on the port side amidships she listed heavily and her speed was reduced to 17 knots. Her end was near, for at 19.15hrs another single aircraft hit her above 'A' boiler room with three bombs. She had by then expended all her 4in ammunition. She was beginning to heel more rapidly and at 20.15hrs rolled right over and sank in lat. 34° 45′ N, long. 23° 12′ E. Captain P. B. R. W. William-Powlett had already given the order to abandon ship. The sun had set* but it was still light enough for a continuance of air attack. The *Kandahar* (Cdr W. G. A. Robson) and *Kingston* (Lt-Cdr P. Somerville) therefore dropped boats and floats, withdrew to the south for forty- five minutes, and returned to the scene after dark. They succeeded in picking up 523 out of a total of 780. Commander W. R. Marshall-A'Deane, who had been picked up by the *Kandahar* after the loss of his destroyer the *Greyhound*, assisted in the rescue work. Seeing a man in difficulties in the water, he dived in and swam to his assistance, but was not seen again. For his gallantry he was posthumously awarded the Albert Medal.

On completion of their rescue of the *Fiji* survivors, the *Kandahar* and *Kingston* shaped course to rejoin King at a rendezvous southward of Crete. With Forces C and A1, King had been steaming to the south-westward all this Thursday afternoon May 22nd, subjected to spasmodic air attacks. At 16.00hrs he was joined by Mountbatten's five destroyers, which had been delayed on passage from Malta by a

* Sunset 20.20hrs. End of nautical twilight 21.23hrs
  Sunrise 06.13hrs. Beginning of nautical twilight 05.10hrs

submarine hunt. Apart from the serious hit on the *Warspite* little damage had been inflicted on the ships which had remained in concentration, but at 16.45hrs the *Valiant* was hit aft by two medium bombs from a high level attack and received slight damage.

At 18.00hrs King's combined Forces C and A1 altered course to the southward. Three hours later an alteration was made to the eastward, their position then being some fifty-five miles south of Crete. In view of the loss that day of the destroyer *Greyhound*, and the two heavy cruisers *Gloucester* and *Fiji*, all in the longitude of Kithera, a feeling was growing that there might be fewer hazards if rallying points were farther east, and that an approach and withdrawal to and from the Aegean might be more feasible at the eastern end of Crete.

Many lessons had been expensively learned on this sad day and it is interesting to read the remarks of the captain of the *Fiji* which, although they now sound so obvious, were learned from bitter experience.

1. Cruisers at high speed and taking full avoiding action can elude a number of dive bombing attacks.

2. The deterrent effect [of AA gunfire] was marked. The 6in particularly caused the dive bombers to release early, and, as ammunition became short, the attacks were pressed further home.

3. Where further intense attack is to be expected . . . extensive rescue operations only endanger further men and ships.

4. Throughout the day, until the very end, no attack approached unobserved: this enabled aircraft to be engaged in good time, and adequate avoiding action to be taken. It was an unobserved attack which finally immobilised *Fiji*. Radar was out of action almost the whole day, and AA lookouts, after a taste of bombing, developed eyes which missed nothing. The danger of low cloud is emphasised.

On this tragic day for the Navy the position ashore in Crete was not a very happy one for the Army. Following the unsuccessful dawn counter-attack to regain control of the Maleme airfield from the Germans, the withdrawal of British troops to a new defensive line farther east was begun. Enemy troop carriers continued to arrive all day at Maleme, though at great cost. In the course of this critical Thursday May 22nd the Germans landed three mountain battalions, parachute artillery, and a field hospital at Maleme: a remarkable achievement considering the state of the airfield and the fact that it was within range of British field guns. There was still no slackening of determination among the gallant defenders, but already towards the end of this third day it was obvious that the Germans had made up considerably for their slow progress on the first two days.

Disembarkation of reinforcements and supplies for the defenders could take place only at night, and approach to and withdrawal from the island had already become hazardous. Nevertheless on the afternoon of Thursday May 22nd, at Alexandria, the special service ship *Glenroy* (Captain Sir James Paget, Bart, ret) embarked 900 men of the Queen's Royal Regiment, the HQ Staff of 16th Infantry Brigade, and eighteen vehicles, and sailed for Tymbaki on the south coast of Crete.

The intention was that Crete must be held, though the position strategically had changed vitally with the loss of the airfield at Maleme. Nowhere was the coast in enemy hands, and all enemy convoys had turned back.

CHAPTER SIX

Alexandria for Replenishment

FRIDAY MAY 23RD

As Friday May 23rd dawned, the ever growing pressure of the German forces in Crete became more evident, and there was considerable harassment of the 5th New Zealand Brigade and of their planned withdrawal which had been impossible to complete under cover of darkness. The German vanguard were already using captured RAF lorries and a Bofors gun with captured ammunition, and endeavouring to break through eastwards. British troops were suffering from shortages due to difficulty of supply and the frequent breakdown of communications.

After the loss of Maleme airfield it became possible to give the Royal Air Force a definite target, and from Friday May 23rd, Marylands, Blenheims, and Wellingtons took a hand in bombing it. They also dropped medical supplies and stores at Heraklion and Retimo. Egyptian-based Hurricanes fitted with extra fuel tanks were also flown to Heraklion for the purpose of attacking Maleme, but the distance factor proved an unavoidable handicap. The whole effort was on too small a scale to be effective, and though scoring many successes the RAF lost many aircraft. The defenders' situation at Heraklion itself was good; the Germans had made little headway, and successful counter-attacks were carried out by British troops. A score or more of troop-carrying aircraft had been destroyed by accurate anti-aircraft fire.

In the early hours of this day Cunningham at Alexandria had been given a false impression about the ammunition situation in ships, due to an error in a 'most immediate' signal made by Rawlings at 22.30hrs/22 the night before. The signal reported the loss of the cruisers *Gloucester* and *Fiji*, and went on to give details of the ammunition situation. As received, the signal made it appear that Rawlings's battleships had no pom-pom ammunition, the word 'empty' having been inadvertently substituted for 'plenty'. This information immediately frustrated the Commander-in-Chief's earlier intention of sending Rawlings's Force A1 to rendezvous with Mountbatten's 5th Destroyer Flotilla, and rather than divide forces or leave small groups in isolation, he decided to recall all ships to Alexandria for replenishment. The signal was made at 04.00hrs/23, and dawn found the various naval forces widely scattered. It must be realised that the transmission of signals involved many technical difficulties and delays and errors in the processes of cyphering and decyphering, especially when signal traffic was swollen. Rawlings stated that throughout these operations the lag was very bad, and suggested that now that the Commander-in-Chief was conducting from shore, far more signal facilities should be provided.

Mountbatten's destroyers *Kelly*, *Kashmir*, *Kipling*, *Kelvin*, and *Jackal* had been detached from the main force at 20.30hrs on the previous evening Thursday May 22nd, and after being instructed to search for survivors in the areas where *Gloucester* and *Fiji* had been lost, were subsequently ordered to enter the Aegean for a night patrol inside Kissamo Bay and Canea Bay. These splendid destroyers had been completed only two years earlier just before war broke out, and were distinctive by virtue of their single funnels. On the way in, upon arrival at the Antikithera Channel, the *Kipling* (Commander A. St Clair-Ford) developed steering trouble and had to be detached to rejoin Force A1. Later on, having overcome the trouble, St Clair-Ford decided to remain to the south-west of Crete so as to be able to rejoin Mountbatten at the appointed rendezvous in the morning after withdrawal from patrol. It is as well that he did, as we shall see.

A signal from Captain J. A. V. Morse, DSO, Naval Officer in Charge at Suda Bay, reported that lights had been seen in Canea Bay, whereupon the *Kelvin* and *Jackal*, having found nothing amiss in Kissamo Bay, were ordered to investigate. The cause proved to be shore lights. These two destroyers then withdrew west-about, and being detached proceeded independently for Alexandria.

The *Kelly* and *Kashmir* had better luck on entering Canea Bay, for they found a caique full of German troops which they immediately attacked. On withdrawing westward they bombarded the enemy-held airfield at Maleme, and engaged and set on fire a second caique.

Earlier this Friday May 23rd at about 0.200hrs, the destroyers *Decoy* and *Hero* had embarked from a village on the south coast no less a person than King George II of Greece, together with members of the Royal Household, in accordance with a plan arranged with NOIC Suda Bay. The King had narrowly escaped from his house at Perivolia shortly before it had been surrounded by Germans, and had made an eventful and difficult two-day journey across the central mountains, escorted by a platoon of New Zealand soldiers, and led by Colonel J. S. Blunt, British military attaché to Greece. As soon as the embarkation from the fishing village of Ayla Roumeli had been completed, *Decoy* and *Hero* sailed to join Force A1.

Following the Commander-in-Chief's order for the fleet withdrawal to Alexandria for replenishment, the naval situation at dawn was a somewhat scattered one. Force D, with Glennie in the *Dido*, was just arriving at Alexandria, and the *Ajax* and *Orion* were some distance astern. Mack of Force E with the destroyers *Jervis, Ilex, Nizam,* and *Havock*, had been patrolling off Heraklion, and having withdrawn through the Kaso Strait was now returning to Alexandria. Prior to the order for withdrawal it had been Cunningham's intention for this force to be strengthened by the cruisers *Ajax* and *Orion*, whose ammunition supply had not been so badly depleted as the *Dido*'s. In the event, his signal ordering this had not been received in time to effect any change in the passage of these ships to Alexandria. Mack was dive-bombed for five hours on his return passage, but the only casualties were the *Ilex* and *Havock*, damaged by near misses.

To the south of Crete at dawn, Rawlings's Force A1 of two battleships and seven destroyers was about twenty-five miles northwest of King's Force C of four cruisers and one destroyer, all well south of Crete and proceeding for Alexandria. At 06.30hrs King was joined by the destroyers *Kandahar* and *Kingston* carrying the *Gloucester* and *Fiji* survivors, both destroyers nearly out of fuel. Upon learning that Force A1 was only twenty-five miles away, King closed Rawlings and fuelled his destroyers from the battleships. *Kandahar* was at this moment down to 10 tons of fuel, *Kingston* 17 tons.

At 07.45hrs, the destroyers *Decoy* and *Hero*, carrying the King of Greece and his household and chief ministers, joined Force A1, and were promptly ordered by Rawlings on to the battleships' screen to ensure that they would not be caught alone by aircraft. In the course of the forenoon all the scattered destroyers rejoined except the *Kelly, Kashmir,* and *Kipling*. Waller in the *Stuart*, with the *Voyager* and *Vendetta*, had been well to the west, having been ordered by Rawlings to search for *Fiji* survivors close to the island of Gaudo. Another

44

group to join the combined forces temporarily were the destroyers *Jaguar* and *Defender*, who had left Alexandria the day before and were taking stores and ammunition for the Army in Crete. After being detached late in the day, they proceeded to Suda Bay arriving at midnight 24.00hrs Friday May 23rd. They spent two hours unloading, and having embarked wounded and men not required, proceeded for Alexandria.

It was mentioned in the last chapter that the special service ship *Glenroy* had sailed for Tymbaki on Thursday afternoon May 22nd, escorted by the anti-aircraft cruiser *Coventry* and the sloops *Auckland* and *Flamingo*. In view of the great naval losses suffered that day, and the general withdrawal ordered on Friday morning at 04.00hrs, Cunningham at 11.17hrs/23 signalled for her recall. This was done after consultation with General Wavell, under the impression that:

'It appeared to be sheer murder to send her on'.★

However the Admiralty regarded her mission in a different light. Cunningham continues:

'At about 16.00hrs to my amazement, the Admiralty sent a direct message to the *Glenroy* ordering her to turn north again, and about an hour later sent me a signal urging that her reinforcements be landed if it could be done that night. Of course it was much too late, so I ordered the *Glenroy* back to Alexandria and informed the Admiralty that if she had proceeded north she would have arrived at daylight, the worst possible time for air attacks with the Luftwaffe everywhere. The less said about this unjustifiable interference by those ignorant of the situation the better.'

It was then agreed that further attempts at reinforcement should be done by the fast minelayer *Abdiel*.

But what of the destroyers of the 5th Destroyer Flotilla that had failed to join the combined forces? Mountbatten with the *Kelly* and *Kashmir* had been withdrawing westward from the Aegean at full speed since dawn, after a successful offensive sweep, and intended joining the *Kipling* south of the island of Gaudo. The ships received two air attacks but suffered no damage. At 07.55hrs/23 however, when thirteen miles south of Gaudo, they were attacked by 24 dive bombers. The *Kipling*, some seven miles to the southward, observed the attack and immediately closed. The *Kashmir*, after dodging

★ *A Sailor's Odyssey*, p 374

45

half-a-dozen bombs, was hit and sank in two minutes. The *Kelly*, at 30 knots under full helm, was hit and turned turtle. After floating upside down for 30 minutes she sank. Dive bombers now machine-gunned, killing or wounding several of the men swimming about. The *Kipling* became the target of six high level bombing attacks, and as each attack developed St Clair-Ford was forced to leave the scene, dodging bombs and firing at her assailants. On one such urgent occasion, with the motor boat in the water but still secured by one of the falls, the boat was dragged under as the *Kipling* got under way, tearing out the davits of the ship, and carrying away the first lieutenant Lt-Cdr J. E. S. Bush, and the first lieutenant of the *Kelly* Lt-Cdr Lord Hugh Beresford; both were trying desperately to cut the falls. The *Kipling* continued her rescue work until 11.00hrs, rescuing 128 officers and men from the *Kelly* including Mountbatten, and 153 from the *Kashmir* including her captain Cdr H. A. King. It was estimated that she was attacked by forty aircraft dropping 83 bombs: an ordeal from which she emerged unscathed. It was a fortunate decision for the *Kelly* and *Kashmir* that had caused St Clair-Ford to wait for them during the night off south-west Crete. At least two enemy aircraft were shot down during these engagements, and at least four were damaged.

At 11.00hrs the gallant little *Kipling* proceeded alone for Alexandria, and continued until she ran right out of fuel the next morning fifty miles from Alexandria. She was met by the *Protector*, which had been sent out to assist her. Here was a case of an isolated ship 'getting away with it', but her good fortune was particularly appropriate in view of the resolution and courage shown by her gallant captain.

On Friday May 23rd, Suda Bay was singled out for attack by German aircraft who concentrated on the five motor torpedo boats and sank them all. The patrol craft *Syvern* was also sunk. These boats together with other light craft had been very active and had certainly accounted for two German aircraft and probably two more. They carried out coastal duties most gallantly, not only search and patrol, but transport of weapons, equipment, and ammunition, and were under almost continuous air attack by day.

A further signal from the Admiralty reached Cunningham this day, made presumably on receipt of the news of Cunningham's order for all ships to withdraw to Alexandria. The signal informed him (and who should know better?) that the outcome of the battle for Crete would have serious repercussions, and that it was vital to prevent seaborne landings in the next day or two, even if further losses resulted. Cunningham replied at some length, stressing the fuel and ammunition situation which existed in practically all ships.

The Chiefs of Staff in London had also asked for an appreciation, to which Cunningham replied that the scale of air attack now made it no longer possible for the Navy to operate in the Aegean, or vicinity of Crete, by day. He could not guarantee to prevent seaborne landings without suffering losses which, added to those already sustained, would seriously prejudice the command of the Eastern Mediterranean.

The Chiefs of Staff replied that the Fleet and the Royal Air Force must accept whatever risk was entailed in preventing considerable enemy reinforcements. If air reconnaissance showed enemy movements by sea north of Crete, the Fleet would have to operate in that area by day, though considerable losses might be expected. Experience would show for how long that situation could be maintained.

The inference concerning experience was particularly hard to take: 'Singularly unhelpful' writes Cunningham, who delayed replying until May 26th.

The 'experience' of the next few days certainly showed that Cunningham was right, as we shall see in the following chapters.

CHAPTER SEVEN

Stretched to the Limit

The aircraft carrier *Formidable* had remained at Alexandria through-out the grim days May 20th–23rd, following her almost continuous use in Mediterranean operations since her arrival in March; these operations had included two hard fought convoys, the battle of Matapan, the bombardment of Tripoli, and the British evacuation from Greece. Her 826 and 829 squadrons of torpedo bomber reconnaissance aircraft, Albacores and Swordfish, had been reduced considerably through action losses, damage, and wear and tear, but her 803 and 806 squadrons of Fulmar fighters had been practically wiped out. Without her fighters and bombers she had become virtually ineffectual as a unit of the fleet.

By Saturday May 24th, Empire Day as it was then known, twelve somewhat patched-up Fulmars had become available, though some were of doubtful reliability. The news reaching us in the *Formidable* was grim, and getting worse as each day passed. We knew that German troops were pouring into Crete, and that the German Luftwaffe dominated the air from the Aegean to Cyrenaica. We knew that our ships had no protection from the air, other than that provided by their own anti-aircraft fire and the ability to manoeuvre at high speed. Lying near us was the badly damaged *Warspite* a visible reminder of recent events. We knew of the loss of the *Juno, Greyhound, Gloucester, Fiji, Kelly,* and the *Kashmir.* We suspected the loss of many old friends and shipmates, and could only hope that there had been numerous survivors from lost ships. News of the safe arrival of the *Kipling* this day was heartening. But we were shocked at the incredible news that the *Hood* had been sunk early that morning by the *Bismarck* in the North Atlantic: the mighty *Hood,* beloved of the whole Navy; large, fast, and powerful. She had been a symbol of Britain's naval might of the 'twenties'.

At dawn on Saturday May 24th the only local forces at sea other than the *Kipling* were the *Jaguar* and *Defender*, returning to Alexandria after their delivery of stores and ammunition at Suda Bay well before dawn, and the *Abdiel* now on outward passage to Suda Bay. The *Abdiel* (Captain the Hon E. Pleydell-Bouverie) had on board two commandos of 'Layforce' and 80 tons of stores. A previous plan to land the special service troops of 'Layforce' on the south-west coast of Crete in the destroyers *Isis*, *Hero*, and *Nizam*, had to be abandoned because of heavy seas on a lee shore.

Cunningham was well aware of the prolonged strain under which his ships were working, and the mounting depression induced by growing losses. The humid weather and low cloud added gloom to the situation. He broadcast the following signal to the Fleet, which raised hopes and stirred desire for immediate action.

'The Army is just holding its own against constant reinforcement of airborne troops. We must *Not* let them down. At whatever cost to ourselves, we must land reinforcements and keep the enemy from using the sea. There are indications that enemy resources are stretched to the limit. We can and must outlast them. *Stick it out.*'

Under these circumstances we were glad to learn that the *Formidable* would be proceeding to sea, and all the evidence of preparation indicated that it could be this day and there was to be a blitz. Following grim news, but with raised hopes, it was better to be up and doing, rather than reduced to pom-pom drill in harbour day after day. In the event a local dust-storm sprang up, and as this would have hazarded the safe arrival of each aircraft of our slender and precious squadrons, sailing was postponed.

On the forenoon of Sunday May 25th, however, *Formidable** sailed, and after flying on the fighter and bomber squadrons in the afternoon, joined the battle squadron which was to be known as Force A now under the command of Vice-Admiral H. D. Pridham-Wippell. This consisted of the two battleships *Queen Elizabeth* (Pridham-Wippell's flagship), and *Barham* and the destroyers *Jervis*, *Janus*, *Kandahar*, *Nubian*, *Hasty*, *Hereward*, *Voyager*, and *Vendetta*.

Because of indications of a possible enemy landing in Sitia Bay at the eastern end of the north coast of Crete, a large force of ships had left Alexandria at 08.00hrs on Saturday May 24th. These were

* *Formidable* (Captain A. W. laT. Bisset); flagship of Rear-Admiral D. W. Boyd, CBE, DSC, Rear-Admiral (Air)

the cruisers *Ajax* (Captain E. D. B. McCarthy, senior officer of the force) and *Dido*, and the destroyers *Imperial*, *Kimberley*, and *Hotspur*. Having passed through the Kaso Strait and swept the north coast during Saturday night without sighting anything, the force withdrew to the southward of Kaso before daylight on Sunday May 25th. The sweep was repeated the next night, but again without incident.

On the evening of Sunday May 25th, following the departure of *Formidable* with Force A under Pridham-Wippell, the *Glenroy* had again sailed from Alexandria, this time with 800 troops on board as reinforcements for Crete. Cunningham was determined that no effort should be spared his replenished ships in the matter of helping the British army in Crete. The *Glenroy*, escorted by the anti-aircraft cruiser *Coventry* and the destroyers *Stuart* and *Jaguar*, had embarked a battalion of the Queen's Regiment which she hoped to land at Tymbaki. During the forenoon of Monday May 26th the force received bombing attacks from enemy reconnaissance aircraft, and at 18.20hrs were subjected to heavy dive bombing and machine-gun attack. One aircraft was shot down and one damaged. The *Glenroy* suffered casualties and slight damage from near misses, and three of her landing craft were rendered useless. Worse still, cased petrol on the upper deck had been set ablaze; an alarming predicament with so many troops on board. The fire however was got under control with the ship being steered down wind, and after a further landing craft had been jettisoned course was resumed to the northward at 19.50hrs. An hour later the *Glenroy* was subjected to an attack by torpedo bombers. All torpedoes were avoided but by now the force was three hours behind schedule, available landing craft had been reduced by a third, and the breaking surf on beaches offered a severe handicap to landing. As soon as it was realised that it would be impossible to land all the troops before daylight it was reluctantly decided to abandon the operation. The force returned to Alexandria. Yet again was the army denied essential supplies and reinforcement.

Although it was realised that the chances of successful transport in slow merchant ships were small, a further attempt was made when convoy AN 31 (two ships escorted by the sloop *Auckland*) left Alexandria at 05.00hrs on Monday May 26th, only to be recalled early the next day.

The *Abdiel* however was again loaded as soon as she returned to Alexandria on Sunday evening May 25th. Having embarked Brigadier R. E. Laycock (the commander of 'Layforce'), 400 men, and 100 tons of stores, she sailed early on Monday May 26th accompanied by the destroyers *Nizam* and *Hero* who also had troops on board. They all arrived safely at Suda during Monday night, and between them were able to land 750 troops and stores. *Abdiel* then embarked 930 of the wounded and men who were no longer required in Crete, and sailed for Alexandria before dawn on Tuesday May 27th, suffering intermittent bombing beginning at daylight when in the Kaso Strait and lasting until 11.30hrs. No severe damage was received except by the *Hero* from a near miss at 07.00hrs which reduced her speed to 28 knots.

While these determined efforts to send in reinforcements were taking place, the spirit of the troops in Crete remained high, in spite of grievous shortages of ammunition, dwindling stocks of food, and an inadequacy of medical arrangements and supplies to cope with the growing number of wounded. And in the fleet there was a renewed spirit of optimism, especially in the *Formidable* when it was learned that there was to be a bombing attack on the airfield at Scarpanto.

Pridham-Wippell's Force A steamed to the north-west at 21 knots. At 02.00hrs in the *Formidable* on Monday May 26th the force and direction of upper winds were deduced, ready for the briefing of pilots at 03.00hrs. The weather was fair and the visibility good. At 03.30hrs the striking force of four Albacores took off as *Formidable* turned into the wind in a position 100 miles south-south-west of Scarpanto. Allowing for wind and bomb load they would reach their target at first light. This force, led by Lieut-Commander G. Saunt, was a very small one compared with the two squadrons of bombers which had been available in the *Formidable* at Matapan just a month earlier. Of the total of eight Albacores ranged for the strike, two could not be flown, and two returned to the carrier owing to unserviceability after take-off.

At 04.30hrs four Fulmar fighters were flown off. With their higher speed they also would reach the target at the beginning of twilight. The airfield at Scarpanto was practically outside the effective range of RAF planes from Egypt, a fact which led the enemy to regard it as immune from attack. They had forgotten about the Fleet Air Arm and the flexibility of attack which an aircraft carrier could provide. Complete surprise was achieved and a number of C.R.42s and Ju87s successfully damaged or destroyed. The limitations brought about by the small number of naval aircraft available greatly reduced the full possibilities of such a strike.

All the *Formidable*'s aircraft had returned safely by 07.00hrs this Monday morning, and we now waited somewhat expectantly for reprisals. In the briefing room our recently returned pilots reported the results of the attack. They very naturally seemed anxious that *Formidable* should get under way at speed from the hornets' nest they had so successfully stirred. Captain McCarthy's cruisers *Ajax* and *Dido* were due to rendezvous with us as soon as they had cleared Kaso Strait on completion of the night patrol off Sitia Bay. His destroyers *Imperial*, *Kimberley*, and *Hotspur* were now on passage to Alexandria for replenishment, having been relieved by the *Napier*, *Kelvin*, and *Jackal*.

On being joined by McCarthy, Pridham-Wippell proceeded southward with his mighty but vulnerable fleet of one aircraft carrier, two battleships, two cruisers, and thirteen destroyers. All would have been well had the carrier had her full quota of fighters, but she was now down to only four serviceable.

As we withdrew to the south, opening the distance from Scarpanto, so we approached the German airfields in North Africa. We were in 'Bomb Alley', and soon we were sighting approaching aircraft on the radar screen. The use of fighters in those days was always a difficult problem, and especially so when they were few. If you launched them too late to allow them to gain height, the enemy bombing attack could develop practically unopposed. If you committed them too early, perhaps on a false scent, the attack could be delayed until the fighters had spent their effort. On this forenoon *Formidable*'s overworked fighters made 24 flights and had twenty combats during which three Stukas were shot down and one damaged. One Fulmar was lost.

At 13.20hrs by which time we were 150 miles from the Kaso Strait a force of about twenty dive bombers were seen on the radar screen, approaching from North Africa. They were greeted by a barrage of fire from the whole fleet in sufficiently open formation to permit ships to take rapid avoiding action. The sky was full of white puffs and brown blobs of smoke. Jagged bits of steel rained into the sea like gigantic hailstones. We were hurtling along at maximum speed, but the noise of the ship's vibration was out-rivalled by the roar of gunfire and the blast and crackle of the pom-poms.

Now we could see the swarm of Stukas in the clear blue sky silhouetted against the bright sunlight. They were already peeling off undaunted by the gunfire. Their target was obviously the carrier.

Violent avoiding action was now taken in answer to the captain's orders for 'Hard a-port' followed next by 'Hard a-starboard'. The *Formidable* responded instantly, heeling sharply to starboard as her head turned to port: then seconds later to port as her head came back again. But all of us on the bridge could see the relentless approach of the Stukas. And now we could hear the whistle of bombs. A mountain of filthy black water shot up close on our starboard bow and rose to eighty feet. Five seconds later there was another mountain, even closer and higher. Millions of crystals of water glittered in the sunlight as they fell. Then there were two in quick succession. We continued to weave. The next one hit. We were immediately on fire on the starboard side forward. A bomb had penetrated one of the 4.5in gun turrets. The explosion had blown out the ship's starboard side below the fo'c'sle causing damage, and the fire appeared to be spreading. The sea was calm and the hull was still sound below the water-line, so little water was being shipped into the great gaping hole as we tore along. The firing from the fleet continued; and still the bombers peeled off to dive. There were further near misses, and then a gigantic jolt in the *Formidable* when the whole ship seemed to lift from aft. A 1,000lb bomb had gone right through the after starboard 4.5in gun sponson and exploded under the starboard quarter. It was an uncanny sensation feeling the stern violently lifted and then falling, shuddering like a tuning-fork vibrating about its fixed end. It was all terrifying yet in some odd way exhilarating. It was also satisfying to be able to realise and to share some of the experiences suffered by our ships during the last six days.

In a while the attack fizzled out. The bombers had withdrawn, doubtless with claims of a carrier and destroyer sunk; for the *Nubian* also had received a bomb hit which had blown her stern off and wiped out her after guns.

Formidable's fire was got under control, and watertight bulkheads sealed off the rest of the ship from the seven compartments which were open to the sea. Our catapult for accelerated take-off was out of action, but we were able to land on two Fulmars, and continued to operate fighters until dark, after which we parted company with Force A and proceeded to Alexandria attended by an anti-submarine screen of four destroyers. The *Nubian* was detached. Escorted by the *Jackal* she was able to return to Alexandria under her own steam, steering on her two screws in the absence of a rudder.

Stick it out? What were our feelings now? For the destruction of a few enemy aircraft and minor damage to Scarpanto airfield, the *Formidable* had been so severely damaged that she would be out of use for several months. We had suffered ten casualties and were once again reduced to half-a-dozen serviceable aircraft. The only carrier in the Eastern Mediterranean was now useless and it would be a very long time before another was available.

News of the damage to the *Formidable* and *Nubian* reached Cunningham while he was writing a reply on Monday May 26th to the Chiefs of Staff message of May 24th which he had found so 'singularly unhelpful'.* To their statement that the Fleet must accept whatever risk was entailed in preventing considerable re-inforcements from reaching Crete, Cunningham** replied:

'It is not the fear of sustaining losses, but the need to avoid losses which will cripple the fleet without any commensurate advantage which is the determining factor in operating in the Aegean. As far as I know the enemy has so far had little success in re-inforcing Crete by sea.

The experience of three days in which two cruisers and four destroyers have been sunk, and one battleship, two cruisers, and four destroyers severely damaged shows what losses are likely to be. Sea control in the Eastern Mediterranean could not be retained after another such experience.'

Cunningham went on to say that the enemy's supply by sea had not yet come into the picture. Enemy reinforcements and stores were able to come in at will by air quite unchecked by any British air action. The sight of a constant and unhindered procession of Ju52s flying into Crete was likely to affect the morale of British troops.

He also stressed the fact that his men and ships were nearing exhaustion, having been kept running almost to the limit of their endurance since the end of February when the decision had been taken to send the British army to Greece.

He complained that he had not received the reconnaissance aircraft he had so earnestly requested. Only adequate air reconnaissance would permit him to keep his ships far enough away by day to avoid serious loss pending the moment when the enemy committed his convoys to sea.

There was yet another casualty the following morning Tuesday

* See Chapter 6, p 43
** *A Sailor's Odyssey*, p 375

May 27th.   At daylight, Pridham-Wippell with Force A, now consisting of the battleships *Queen Elizabeth* and *Barham*, and the destroyers *Jervis*, *Janus*, *Kelvin*, *Napier*, *Kandahar*, and *Hasty*, were 250 miles south-east of Kaso, steering to the north-westward, and about to detach the cruisers *Ajax* and *Dido* to Alexandria. *Formidable* had safely reached Alexandria and had entered harbour at 07.00hrs on this Tuesday morning.   The *Glenroy* and her escort lay some distance to the north-west of Force A, and were steering for Alexandria following an abortive attempt to land troops at Tymbaki. In Kaso Strait were the *Abdiel*, *Hero*, and *Nizam* returning to Alexandria from Suda.   Somewhere in between was the convoy AN 31 shortly to be recalled to Alexandria when her mission to Crete was cancelled.

At daylight Pridham-Wippell had altered course for the Kaso Strait to cover *Abdiel*'s withdrawal.   Three hours later at 08.59hrs, Force A was attacked by fifteen Stukas approaching from the direction of the sun.   The *Barham* was hit on Y turret, and two of her bulges were flooded by near misses; two aircraft were shot down and one was seen to be damaged.   A fire started in the *Barham* and grew rapidly until course was altered to steer down wind: even then it was not extinguished for two hours.

At 12.30hrs on Tuesday May 27th Cunningham ordered Force A to return to Alexandria.

In the meantime there had been some very hard fighting in Crete, with German pressure increasing daily in the region between Maleme and Canea.   General Ringel, commanding the 5th Mountain Division, had taken command of 'Group West' which spent Saturday May 24th preparing for a general assault eastward to break the new defensive line which ran from the north coast southward through the village of Galatas into the hills, a line roughly three miles west of Canea.

Ringel's troops, by now swollen to 15,000, had mortars and air co-operation.   The forenoon was spent in 'softening up' from the air. By the afternoon of Sunday May 25th the Germans had taken Galatas and broken through the defensive line composed of only about 6,000 New Zealanders, Australians, and Greeks, all of whom had been at the mercy of air attack for several days.   The situation was restored by a bold and brilliant counter-attack with bayonets, ordered and led by Colonel H. K. Kippenberger of the 10th New Zealand Brigade.   Galatas was re-taken by two companies and two light tanks of the 3rd Hussars, affording a respite to the defending troops for withdrawal to stronger positions ready for renewed attack. Here was certainly a case of 'stretched to the limit', but in spite of the prolonged bombardment and lack of reinforcements the defenders fought with resolution and gallantry, and there were many notable deeds. The names of two who won the Victoria Cross for repeated acts of great courage were 2nd Lieutenant C. H. Upham, 20th New Zealand Battalion, and Sergeant A. C. Hulme, 23rd New Zealand Battalion.

General Freyberg described Kippenberger's counter-attack as 'one of the great efforts in the defence of Crete'. But by then he had come to the conclusion that it could be only a matter of time before Crete was lost. On Monday May 26th the situation in the Suda area rapidly worsened. Air attack was incessant and the Germans succeeded in working round the southern flank. Freyberg sent a message to General Wavell informing him that the troops in the western sector had reached the limits of their endurance after the continual fighting and concentrated bombing of the past seven days. Asministration was extremely difficult (owing to a breakdown of communication) but if evacuation were decided upon at once it would be possible to bring off a part of the force, though not all.

Freyberg was determined to hold the Suda area as long as possible, so that ships bringing reinforcements could be unloaded; the *Abdiel*, *Hero*, and *Nizam* were due to arrive at midnight. He also gave orders for a planned retreat to Sphakia on the south coast, to begin on Tuesday May 27th. His plan involved much regrouping in order to safeguard Suda and at the same time to hold the area south-west of Canea. A rearguard under Major-General E. C. Weston, composed of Royal Marines and Anzac troops, would absorb the Layforce commandos landing at Suda. Considerable delays in transmission of orders resulted from the breakdown of communication, resulting in confusion and misunderstanding, and the collapse of the Canea front. The task now fell to the rearguard to hold back the Germans as long as possible, to permit withdrawal of our troops southward across the mountains to Sphakia.

Late on the night of Monday May 26th, Wavell replied to Freyberg advising him to hold on as long as he could. He told him of a cable received from the Prime Minister which said:

'Victory in Crete essential. Keep hurling in all you can'.

It was already too late. That same day, the Commander-in-Chief of each of the three services, Cunningham, Wavell, and Tedder, had met General Blamey* and Mr Fraser**, both of whom were gravely concerned as to the fate of the Anzac troops fighting so desperately in Crete. Evacuation was the topic. Could the troops be withdrawn safely or would surrender become inevitable? Cunningham† made it quite clear that 'Whatever the risks, whatever our losses, the remaining ships of the fleet would make an all-out effort to bring away the Army'. But he warned Wavell that the moment might come when terrible losses could be inflicted from the air; to save numerous lives, surrender might then be more humane. Tedder promised all available help that could be raised from the RAF in the Middle East.

On Monday May 26th the Argyll and Sutherland Highlanders and two of the I tanks which had been landed with them at Tymbaki a week earlier, succeeded in breaking through to join the British troops who had repulsed and slaughtered thousands of attacking German paratroopers in the Heraklion region, and were still holding out. These troops had formed the original garrison in Crete, and were far better equipped than those British and Imperial troops who had taken over the defence of the Maleme-Suda area after their evacuation from Greece only a month before. The position at Heraklion was however clearly untenable, and could have little effect on the fighting going on 50 or 60 miles to the west. It was only a matter of time before they would be cut off.

At Retimo also, the Germans had made little headway against a gallant and determined resistance, but by Monday May 26th the defenders were cut off and were short of rations and ammunition. Freyberg made several efforts to inform the senior officer Colonel I. R. Campbell of the situation in the west, and that he was to withdraw to Plaka Bay on the south coast. The information never got through.

But there was one piece of heartening news that reached us at Alexandria on Tuesday May 27th. This was of the sinking of the German battleship *Bismarck* which had sunk HMS *Hood* three days earlier. She had been successfully hunted in prolonged operations

---

* General Sir Thomas Blamey, General Officer Commanding Australian Forces in the Middle East.
** Rt Hon Peter Fraser, Prime Minister of New Zealand.
† *A Sailor's Odyssey*, p 378

involving many British ships. History is full of incidents where the hunted ship slips through the net of overwhelming strength, but in this case the *Bismarck* had been fairly caught and forced to pay the inevitable penalty. This was particularly encouraging news after all our recent heavy losses in the Mediterranean and the grim reality that Crete was as good as lost.

CHAPTER EIGHT

Retreat from Suda

In a message originated at 08.24hrs on Tuesday May 27th, General Wavell replied to the Prime Minister's instructions to 'keep hurling in all you can'. He informed him that the Canea front had collapsed, and that Suda Bay could be covered for only twenty-four hours more. It was no longer possible to land reinforcements because of the complete German domination of the air. He deeply regretted the failure. But to prolong the defence further would merely exhaust the resources of all three services, and gravely compromise the defence of the Middle East.*

The Chiefs of Staff replied at once, authorising evacuation. As many men as possible were to be saved without regard to material.

'And so we wearily turned to planning another evacuation', wrote Cunningham, 'with fewer ships, far less resources . . . and our seamen and ships worn to the point of exhaustion.'

'But it has to be remembered', said Cunningham in his despatch, 'that the Navy's duty was achieved and no enemy ship, whether warship or transport, succeeded in reaching Crete.' Neither were the Navy's operational intentions foiled at any stage by the Italian fleet.

The fact that the retreat to Sphakia had already begun, lessened in no degree the need for fighting. On Tuesday May 27th there was a sharp encounter with the Germans near Suda, followed by a determined counter-attack by the 5th New Zealand and 19th Australian Brigades. This well-conducted response caused heavy casualties in the German 141st Mountain Regiment. Using bayonets a Maori battalion particularly distinguished itself and relieved pressure decisively. Although the Germans established themselves in Canea that day, and occupied much of the ground to the south-east, all

---

* It should be remembered that among Wavell's other anxieties at this time were Rommel's growing Afrika Korps threat to Egypt, and increasing German interest in Syria and Iraq.

thought of their reaching the town of Suda had to be abandoned.

At Suda, Captain Morse the NOIC now shared headquarters with General Freyberg under a tree in a gully near Suda Point, preparing for withdrawal to Sphakia. They reckoned to have 1,000 men at Sphakia ready for embarkation on the following night, Wednesday May 28th, and larger numbers on succeeding nights, priority being given to wounded men. On Tuesday May 27th, Morse had sent a radio set in Motor Launch 1011 which was to proceed during the night for Sphakia, as that place would be the site of final headquarters, and must be in communication with headquarters at Alexandria. The motor launch was delayed by heavy seas, took shelter, and was spotted after dawn by aircraft and sunk. The radio was lost, but the crew were able to swim ashore, and walk over the mountains to Sphakia, guided by Greeks.

Withdrawal from Suda necessitated the dispersal of the local small craft that had been there since the withdrawal from Greece. In the words of Morse, referring in particular to the corvette *Salvia* (Lieut-Cdr J. I. Miller, DSO, RNR) and the mine-sweeper *Lanner* (Skipper W. Stewart, RNR), they went about their hazardous duties in a 'fearless and determined' manner. It is only fair to add that all the vessels of the Crete Patrol Force performed resolute service, in spite of being repeatedly and heavily bombed and machine-gunned. In addition to the motor torpedo boats already mentioned in an earlier chapter, and the *Salvia* and *Lanner*, there were the mine-sweepers *Widnes* (Lieut-Cdr R. B. Chandler, RN), *Derby* (Lt F. C. V. Brightman, RN), and the trawler *Moonstone* (Lieut-Cdr P. G. Britten, RNR); four South African-built whalers *Syvern* (Lieut-Cdr R. E. Clarke, RNR), KOS 21 (Lieut-Cdr I. H. Wilson, SAN), KOS 22 (Lieut H. D. Foxon, RNR), KOS 23 (Lieut-Cdr L. J. Reid, RNVR); and three motor launches 1011 (Lt A. H. Blake, RNR), 1030 (Lt W. M. O. Cooksey, RNVR), and 1032 (Lt E. N. Rose, RNVR). There were also three A lighters under the command of Lt B. W. Waters, RNVR, used for the transport of trucks, light tanks, and motor vehicles.

At midnight on Monday May 26th all the remaining patrol craft were ordered to sail for Suda and proceed west-about for Alexandria. The ML 1011 had already left, only to be sunk with the precious radio set the next morning. Of the other two motor launches,

Diagram 3. (*Opposite*) The withdrawal route from Suda to Sphakia.

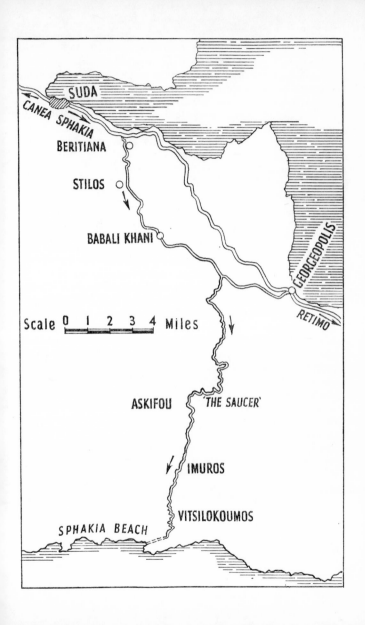

SUDA
CANEA SPHAKIA
BERITIANA
STILOS
BABALI KHANI
GEORGEOPOLIS
RETIMO
Scale 0 1 2 3 4 Miles
ASKIFOU 'THE SAUCER'
IMUROS
VITSILOKOUMOS
SPHAKIA BEACH

ML 1032 survived a 20-minute duel with an aircraft and arrived safely at Alexandria, but ML 1030 was bombed and sunk fifteen miles west of the island of Gaudopula. The crew of ML 1030 took to the dinghy and a raft, under a withering machine-gun fire, and rowed and baled for twenty hours, the dinghy towing the raft in a heavy sea. Arrived at the island they plugged the bullet holes in the dinghy and set off for a 20-mile pull to Crete, eventually arriving safely at Sphakia. The *Salvia, Moonstone, Derby, Widnes*, and KOS 23 had all been withdrawn from Suda for service elsewhere on Tuesday May 20th, the last two being bombed and sunk.

From his makeshift gully headquarters, shared with Freyberg, Morse sent a truck to the dock area to collect remaining provisions before withdrawing. The truck was machine-gunned and burnt out, and of the occupants Lieut-Cdr I. G. Robertson was seriously wounded, and Leading Seaman Simonite killed.

At 21.00hrs that day Tuesday 27th May, Morse ordered the signal station to be destroyed, and a portable radio set to be loaded into a truck destined for Sphakia. At 22.00hrs a small convoy of lorries with Freyberg and Morse and a skeleton staff started for Sphakia. Progress over the single congested mountain road was slow and bumpy. The jolting damaged the radio valves, and the radio set soon became unserviceable. The headquarters of withdrawing troops was now out of touch with Middle East Command Headquarters and the Naval Headquarters at Alexandria. Morse however knew of yet another radio set which had originally belonged to an RAF unit, and had already been sent to Sphakia. He found it in a cave about a mile from Sphakia. By 10.00hrs on Wednesday May 28th this cave had been established as a rudimentary headquarters, and radio communication with Alexandria and Middle East headquarters had been restored.

Freyberg was concerned about the difficulty of breaking contact with the enemy, and requested that embarkation should be expedited. He was doubtful if General Weston could hold off the enemy pursuit even for two more days. On Wednesday May 28th however there was a successful rearguard action by the 5th New Zealand Brigade at Stilos, seven miles from Suda along the rugged mountainous way to Sphakia. On this same day the main body of 'Layforce' and the 2/8th Australian Battalion held off two attacks by the 85th Mountain Regiment at Babali Khani, eleven miles from Suda. They had the benefit of one of the very few remaining I tanks, and were able to hold on all day in a well chosen position which prevented the Germans from making effective use of their own artillery. The 'Layforce' stand thus blocked the route to Sphakia and Retimo, for there was a road fork to both places four miles farther on.

Isolated pockets of men had been captured by the Germans prior to these stands, but there was small risk of this happening on this rough narrow route as long as the rearguard could hold out. Small counter-attacks by 'Layforce' at dusk effectively discouraged the Germans from attempting any night operation. It had been noted that the absence of close support by the Luftwaffe in this hilly country denied the enemy the considerable backing they had enjoyed hitherto.

The 4th New Zealand Brigade had been sent farther back to a place called Askifou, twenty-five miles from Suda, and only eight miles from Sphakia. At this point there was a plateau or saucer of about a mile in diameter, and it had been seen as a possible landing place for German paratroops in an attempt to head off the retreat. German air activity was however on a diminished scale in this area on this day, and concentrated for preference on the expected break out from Retimo and Heraklion. The occasional aircraft would arrive to rake the path with fire, and men would fall flat or take shelter beneath boulders; alternatively they might lie up during the day in shelter and resume the retreat at night-time. Discipline varied. Combatant units generally proceeded in orderly fashion, but there were also disorganised rabbles of men often without arms of any description. As the men got nearer to their destination, the road became rougher, leading to precipitous slopes and a blotting out of path. They were hungry, short of water, their boots were broken and cut, and many were near exhaustion. The retreat was becoming a test of endurance.

Beneath it all there seemed to be a confidence, a certainty that once they reached Sphakia the end of the road was near. The Navy would be there to take them off. Somebody would fix it. We shall see how the Navy fared.

There is a story that in the midst of this long trail of retreating men there was a young girl holding a rifle, and resting by the road-side. She looked no more than seventeen and had long blonde hair. The men stared at her in curiosity, but were too weary even to comment. One man however, with a week's growth on his grimy face, raised a hand in salutation as he passed.

63

CHAPTER NINE

Navy to the Rescue

WEDNESDAY MAY 28TH–THURSDAY MAY 29TH

In spite of grave losses, severe damage, accumulating defects, and no time for overhaul or repair, Cunningham's ships were ready to face the supreme task of getting troops off Crete and bringing them to Alexandria. It was estimated that there were some 22,000 to be evacuated, and with German reinforcements arriving in ever increasing numbers, and growing pressure, the prospects of rescuing more than a small proportion did not seem high. Speed was essential, and it was vital to know exactly where the retreating troops could be embarked and in what numbers. Cunningham had been out of radio touch with the sequence of operations in the withdrawal from Suda, owing to the breakdown of the radio link, during the period from 21.00hrs Tuesday May 27th when the signal station had been abandoned, until the forenoon of Wednesday May 28th when Morse had set up headquarters in a cave at Sphakia. Before the breakdown however, Morse in his last message from Suda had given an estimate of the numbers expected to be available for embarkation during the next four nights from Heraklion in the north, and from Sphakia, Plaka, and Tymbaki in the south. These figures proved to be substantially correct and enabled the necessary plans to be made at Alexandria, and an allocation of the right number of ships as far as possible. Now that opposition by the defenders had virtually ceased, it was expected that the Luftwaffe would make an all-out effort on ships at sea. Except for the brief period of *Formidable*'s operation against Scarpanto airfield, the fleet had been without fighter defence. The RAF had however now promised some fighter cover, though this could be only spasmodic owing to the great distances involved. Group Captain C. B. R. Pelly was attached temporarily to Cunningham's staff at Alexandria to co-ordinate the operation of RAF fighters with the movements of ships. A military liaison officer Major-General J. F. Evetts was also attached.

Cunningham paid warm tribute to the close co-ordination achieved by these two officers.

The plan was that embarkation of troops should be confined to the three hours immediately following midnight, in order to allow ships four hours of darkness on each side of this period, for steaming, and to be as far as possible from enemy air bases during the hours of daylight. Troops from the Suda area would come off at Sphakia, and those from Heraklion were to embark at Heraklion harbour. Those from Retimo could most easily retreat to Plaka, and be taken off by HM ships calling in there, but in the event it was not possible to issue instructions as there was no radio link with the defending troops at Retimo, nor had these troops received news of the evacuation generally. On Thursday May 29th an RAF aircraft flew over Retimo and dropped a message phrased in slang so as to be unintelligible if picked up by the Germans, ordering withdrawal to Plaka. It is apparent that it was never received, for the commanding officer Lieut-Colonel I. R. Campbell continued the defence of the airfield until Friday May 30th when, with ammunition and rations spent, he was forced to surrender. Of the 1,000 who had composed the Retimo garrison, 160 were killed in action, 140 escaped into the wilds of the island, and 700 were taken prisoner, none realising that rescue would be available just ten miles away on the south coast.

At Sphakia some of the difficulties of embarkation from the small shingle beach became apparent to Freyberg and Morse, after they had established headquarters in a cave during the forenoon of Wednesday May 28th. One of the chief needs for a beachmaster controlling traffic at the final embarkation is rapid communication between the embarkation point and the feeding points. In this case touch between the beach area and the top of the escarpment could be maintained only by messengers on foot, and the journey would take an active man two hours. The road over the mountains finished in acute hairpin bends and then ended abruptly at the top of a 500-foot cliff from which a goat track led down to the beach and a small fishing village. The beach was under 200 yards in length and only 20 yards in depth, which greatly restricted the numbers that could be assembled. By daylight troops had to remain hidden from air observation whether on the plateau or on the beach, and yet be ready in controlled numbers to be taken off as soon as warships' boats touched down on the beach that night. How long it would be before the men awaiting embarkation might be over-run by the advancing Germans, depended on the skill and gallantry of the rearguard. As the time element became an increasingly important factor, and hunger and thirst grew, so the number of 'gate crashers' grew. The main concern of the Germans on this day however seemed to be to cut off the Heraklion garrison who had been so successful, and to capture the airfield which was still in the defenders' hands.

As for the ships which were to embark the troops, Cunningham described them as having been driven hard for more than two months without respite. Their number was depleted and machinery had become unreliable. Officers and men were on the verge of complete exhaustion, physically and mentally.

At 06.00hrs on Wednesday May 28th, less than 24 hours after the decision to evacuate, and an hour or two before Morse had established his radio link in a cave at Sphakia, two cruisers and six destroyers sailed from Alexandria for Heraklion harbour. This was Force B, under Rawlings, flying his flag in the *Orion* accompanied by the cruisers *Ajax* and *Dido*, and the destroyers *Decoy*, *Jackal*, *Imperial*, *Hotspur*, *Kimberley*, and *Hereward*. Their object was to embark the whole of the Heraklion garrison of 4,000 that night.

Two hours later, four destroyers sailed from Alexandria carrying additional boats for beach work off Sphakia, and small arms and provisions for those troops who could not be embarked that night. This was Force C, under Captain S. H. T. Arliss in the destroyer *Napier* accompanied by the *Nizam*, *Kelvin*, and *Kandahar*.

The two forces on their missions of mercy were to have vastly different experiences, perhaps because of the German preoccupation over the stubbornness of the Heraklion defenders. Arliss arrived off Sphakia without incident in time to begin embarkation at 00.30hrs on Thursday May 29th. By 03.00hrs his force had taken off nearly 700 men, and had landed the urgently needed rations for the 15,000 yet to come. Among the *Napier*'s passengers were three women, one Chinaman, two children and a dog. Fighter protection had been requested for 05.45hrs. Nevertheless at 09.00hrs the force was attacked by four Ju88s and the *Nizam* was narrowly missed, suffering minor damage but no reduction in speed. A crashed enemy aircraft was sighted at 09.40hrs, having probably been shot down by RAF fighters. At 17.00hrs on Thursday May 29th, Force C entered harbour at Alexandria with the first group of survivors from Crete.

This augured well, but there was as yet no news of the arrival of Force B from Heraklion.

It had been the intention that the whole force of 4,000 should be brought off from Heraklion in one lift; hence the size of Force B. Having left Alexandria at 06.00hrs on Wednesday May 28th, steering at speed for the Kaso Straits, Rawlings encountered nothing until 17.00hrs/28 when, ninety miles from Scarpanto, his force was subjected to a series of air attacks from high level bombers, dive bombers, and torpedo bombers. These attacks continued till after sunset. At 19.20hrs/28 the *Imperial* (Lieut-Cdr C. A. DeW. Kitcat) received a near miss but appeared to be undamaged: in fact she had sustained damage to her steering which was to have grave consequences later in the operation. At 20.10hrs/28 the *Ajax* received a near miss and sustained damage and casualties which were reported to Rawlings, who at once ordered her back to Alexandria. Subsequent examination revealed that the damage was not so serious as at first reported, and she could have safely continued with Force B. It was the *Imperial* that should have returned, not *Ajax*, but Rawlings was not to know at that time, and did what he thought best to avoid keeping a lame duck that would retard progress.

Rawlings arrived off Heraklion at 23.30hrs/28. His destroyers immediately entered harbour and went alongside the main jetty to take off the allocated number of troops and transfer them to the cruisers waiting outside. Rawlings later commended as admirable the embarkation arrangements that had been made ashore by the NOIC Heraklion, Captain M. H. S. MacDonald. By 03.20hrs on Thursday May 29th the whole of the Heraklion garrison, amounting to some 4,000 troops, had been smoothly embarked, an operation performed in complete darkness, and without alarming the enemy. The rearguard (the York and Lancasters) had had to hold a covering position to the end, and break off in small numbers causing delay. The only indignant soldier was the commander of the garrison Brigadier B. H. Chappel, who claimed that he had won his battle. Indeed he had, but it was later learned that a big German assault was in preparation for the capture of Heraklion airfield on the afternoon of Thursday May 29th. By such a narrow margin was the evacuation at Heraklion completed. But they still had the long journey to Alexandria. The embarkation had taken almost four hours, and there was concern as every minute after 03.00hrs passed, that they might not be clear of the Kaso Straits before the coming dawn.

At 03.20hrs/29 however the squadron proceeded to sea working quickly up to 29 knots. Most of the troops were soon asleep in spite of their cramped quarters on the mess decks below. The congestion can be imagined when it is realised for example that the *Orion* was now carrying 1,100 troops in addition to her complement of 550 officers and men, and the destroyers 300 in addition to their ship's complement of 150 officers and men.

The squadron had just reached maximum speed, steaming in formation for the Straits at 03.45hrs, when *Imperial*'s steering gear failed, and her rudder jammed. Quite out of control, she narrowly missed colliding with the *Kimberley* and the two cruisers. Rawlings had to make a quick decision. He could wait while *Imperial* diagnosed the trouble and if possible put it right, meanwhile imperilling the whole squadron and the 4,000 troops; or he could abandon her after removing the troops. He decided on the latter and flashed a signal to the *Hotspur* (Lieut-Cdr C. P. F. Brown) 'Take off crew and sink *Imperial*', adding, as the squadron resumed passage, 'Make for Alexandria'. Cunningham later remarked that this decision could not be cavilled at, but he thought it might have been wiser to remove the troops only, and let ship and crew take their chance on a struggle home.

It was the belief in the *Hotspur* that this was now to be their own fate. Transfer of troops would take up another precious hour. With the coming dawn they were likely to be alone in the Kaso Straits, no more than thirty miles from the enemy airfield in Scarpanto. Officers and men of both the *Imperial* and *Hotspur* realised the desperate urgency of the occasion. With Rawlings proceeding eastward at 30 knots for the turn southward at the Kaso Straits, every ten minutes would take his squadron five miles farther away. *Hotspur* was soon secured alongside *Imperial*, and every possible gangway was got out. Most of the troops had to be awakened and got up to the upper deck for transfer, and many of the crew of the *Imperial* found time to collect their more precious possessions in a suit-case before abandoning their ship. Soon *Hotspur* stood off. A torpedo was fired. *Imperial* heeled over, then righted, settling low in the water. A second torpedo was fired. This time she turned over and settled slowly into the dark water. The irony and heartburning at having to sink this fine destroyer, recently refitted, can be imagined. It was now 04.45hrs, only a few minutes before the beginning of twilight. With a total of 900 men on board (600 troops plus two destroyer complements) *Hotspur* now worked up to full speed and steamed eastward for the north-east corner of Crete. A whole precious hour had been lost, and by now Rear-Admiral Rawlings must be thirty miles farther on.

As the grey light of dawn crept over the scene, the crews turned to their guns and got up ammunition. The first lieutenant of the *Hotspur* (Lieut-Cdr H. Hodgkinson) mustered willing soldiers who had Bren guns, tommy guns, anti-tank guns, and even rifles, to station themselves on the upper deck. The risk of being machine-gunned by attacking aircraft was great, but no greater than that of receiving a bomb on the mess deck where hundreds of troops were congregated. The captain had already decided that if they were to be alone they might stand more of a chance if they hugged the coast, keeping off the normal track to Alexandria.

In the process of hugging the coast and passing inside a small island near the north-east point of Crete, so as to cut the corners, indistinct grey shapes were suddenly seen in the twilight. It could be an Italian squadron. As the light grew behind the dark masses, the silhouettes of British ships were recognised. Rawlings had proceeded at a reduced speed of only 15 knots.

'It's the *Orion*' went up the cry. The utter relief is described in Hugh Hodgkinson's *Turn of the Tide*[*]:

'Never have I been so "pro" anybody as I was pro-Rawlings at that moment. We did not know him well, but on hearing about him later one realised that Rawlings could never leave an un-damaged ship in the lurch if he could get there to add his support. It was Rawlings who had taken the battleships into the Kithero Channel to save the cruisers, and now he had reduced speed and waited for us.'

The *Hotspur* was ordered to take the wing position on the starboard side of the destroyer screen. It was 06.00hrs, and the squadron was now steaming southward through the Kaso Straits: 300 miles to go to Alexandria; a passage of at least ten hours, half of which would be within bombing range of the Stukas.

Fighter protection at 05.30hrs had been requested, and this was confirmed by the Commander-in-Chief the night before. There was however no sign of RAF fighters as yet, and at 06.00hrs four Ju88s appeared, silhouetted against the eastern sky like birds of ill

[*] Published by Harrap, 1944

omen. At 06.00hrs the dive bombing began. Sometimes the attacks were concentrated on the two cruisers *Orion* and *Dido*, sometimes on individual ships of the destroyer screen. A hail of gunfire met every attack. Hodgkinson describes it vividly as seen from the *Hotspur*:

'Down they came screaming out of the half-light one after the other. The Captain stood on the bridge. He had already been there 24 hours. As the leader turned vertically down on us from starboard, he swung the destroyer hard over to starboard, and for the next seven hours he drove us with amazing precision, watching each bomber as a cat would watch a bird, and then, as they dived on us, he would throw the *Hotspur* hard over towards them, so as to force them to be diving steeper and steeper on the way down, which tended to make them pull out early to avoid getting past the vertical . . . As a result, none of the Stukas dived in really close, but shied and pulled out above 2,000 feet at which height they were inaccurate, and all missed us.'

No sooner had the dive bombers completed their attack than they would return to Scarpanto for reloading, unworried by fuelling problems for the few miles involved.

At 06.25hrs one bomber, perhaps more courageous than others, dived steeply during an attack on the *Hereward* (Lieut-Cdr W. J. Munn) in the port wing of the screen. She was seen to be hit amidships, suffered an immediate reduction of speed, and fell away astern of the squadron. Rawlings was forced once again to make a quick decision. Should he stand by the *Hereward*, thus gravely imperilling the rest of his squadron and the troops on board, or must he adopt the harder line of abandoning her to her fate? He chose the latter, a decision later endorsed by Cunningham as undoubtedly correct. When last seen the *Hereward* was making slowly for the coast of Crete, her guns firing as enemy aircraft closed for the final despatch. A large number of survivors were picked up by Italian motor-boats and were made prisoner.

Rawlings continued southward at 30 knots still hopeful of fighter protection. At 06.45hrs however the *Decoy* received a near miss which affected her speed, and Rawlings was now compelled to reduce to 25 knots. At 07.30hrs a bomb fell very close to the *Orion*, causing a further reduction of the speed of the squadron to 21 knots. The position was taking on an ugly appearance, and became grimmer when Rawlings received a signal from RAF HQ 204 Group indicating that there had been confusion over zone-times. The signal promised that fighters would contact him at 05.40hrs GMT. But Rawlings had asked for fighters to contact his force from 05.40hrs (local time) onwards: ie 05.40hrs (− 3) in Zone minus 3. This grave error somewhere in transmission meant that Rawlings could not now expect fighter support until 08.40hrs (local time) unless his urgent signals produced results. Meanwhile matters were getting worse, in spite of the enthusiasm among those many soldiers who fired their Bren guns and Lewis guns from the upper decks of the various ships, to deter the attackers. Some of the attackers were more resolute than others. Soon after 07.30hrs a Stuka raked the *Orion*'s bridge, mortally wounding Rawling's flag captain, G. R. B. Back, and also slightly wounding Rawlings. Back died two hours later, and command of the *Orion* then passed to Commander T. C. T. Wynne. By this time the *Orion* had been hit on A turret and set on fire, and in the *Dido* (Captain H. W. V. McCall) B turret had been completely destroyed by a bomb.

A lull in the assault enabled fire parties to clear away damage and put out fires, while medical staff dealt with the wounded. But just as hopes were raised that attackers had been fought off, there was a renewed onslaught. This time, 10.45hrs, a wave of eleven Ju87s dived in succession on the *Orion*, determined to sink her. Almost hidden by smoke and towering splashes, she emerged still able to steam, but evidently badly hit and temporarily out of control. The results of this hit were appalling, for a bomb had passed through the bridge to explode below on the stokers' mess deck where the space was crowded with soldiers, of whom there were in all 1,100 on board. Casualties amounted to 260 killed, 280 wounded. To add to the disaster there were blazing fires, and damage to compasses, steering gear, and engine room telegraphs. Many compartments were in darkness.

The first lieutenant had been killed, but his duties were quickly assumed by the captain of the corvette *Salvia* (Lieut-Cdr J. I. Miller, DSO, DSC, RD, RNR) who organised fire and rescue parties. He had been specially included in this evacuation operation because of his expert knowledge of Heraklion harbour and the coastal water of Crete. The engine room department also distinguished themselves, in spite of losing three engineer officers killed. Oil fuel had become contaminated with salt water when three of the boiler rooms were damaged, nevertheless an average of 21 knots was maintained, and all fires were got under control.

The squadron were now 100 miles from Kaso, with only 200 to go. A lull in the attacks gave hope again that the attackers were a spent force, or at this distance less able to find their prey despite the clear weather. Still there was no sign of RAF fighters, but at noon two naval Fulmars were due. They arrived punctually, having been sent by the Commander-in-Chief with orders to stay with Rawlings until their fuel was exhausted, when they should 'ditch' and be picked up by destroyers. At such large distances from base their operational time over the squadron was greatly limited. In the event it was found possible to relieve them before their fuel ran out.

It was sad that none of the RAF fighters was seen over the squadron this day. Several abortive attempts had been made to find the ships, which only serves to illustrate the oft made claim of the Navy when fighting for control and training of its own Fleet Air Arm for so many years; the claim that naval aviation can be undertaken effectively only by naval trained airmen. This applies particularly to navigation, reconnaissance, and identification. The RAF had gallantly sent out fighters, and although they were unable to find our ships they shot down two Ju88s for the loss of one Hurricane. The RAF had also sent eight Wellingtons early this day to bomb Scarpanto, but the great distance of their objective seriously handicapped the results it was hoped to achieve.

There were no further dive bombing attacks on Rawlings's force during the afternoon of this long, trying, tragic Thursday May 29th. Three high level bomb attacks took place at 13.00hrs, 13.30hrs, and 15.00hrs, without effecting any further damage. The greatest concern now was whether the *Orion* would make port. Her list appeared to increase, and she would occasionally belch yellow smoke and decrease speed, as her fuel became further contaminated with the sea-water getting into her oil tanks.

But at 20.00hrs that evening Force B eventually arrived at Alexandria. *Orion* then had only two rounds of 6in H.E. ammunition left, and but 10 tons of fuel. Cunningham described the scene:[*]

'Rawlings brought his shattered squadron into Alexandria . . . I shall never forget the sight of those ships coming up harbour, the guns of their fore-turrets awry, one or two broken off and pointing

[*] *A Sailor's Odyssey*, p 384

forlornly skyward, their upper decks crowded with troops, and the marks of their ordeal only too plainly visible. I went on board at once and found Rawlings cheerful but exhausted. The ship (*Orion*) was a terrible sight and the mess deck a ghastly shambles.'

Of the 4,000 soldiers taken off at Heraklion at the beginning of this long day, 800 had been killed, wounded, or (in the case of those in the *Hereward*) captured. Not many more than three thousand soldiers had been rescued, with the substantial loss of many seamen and stokers and two destroyers, and the sustaining of damage to the *Orion* and *Dido* which would keep them out of service for months. Perhaps not much in practical achievement, but it was still possible to boast of an unbroken tradition. The Navy had kept its pledge 'not to let the Army down'.

CHAPTER TEN

Beyond the Limit

We have seen that ships had been got ready to sail from Alexandria for the evacuation as early as Wednesday May 28th: Force C, with Arliss, bound for Sphakia; Force B, with Rawlings, bound for Heraklion. Later that same day at 21.00hrs Force D, under King, also sailed for Sphakia.

Although only 700 had been taken off from Sphakia by Arliss's four destroyers in the early hours of Thursday May 29th, Morse's estimate had been that there would be 10,000 troops ready for embarkation the next day, Friday May 30th, moreover this would have to be the last night of evacuation, as it was unlikely that the Germans could be held back much longer.

Force D consisted of the two cruisers *Phoebe* and *Perth*, two anti-aircraft cruisers *Calcutta* and *Coventry*, three destroyers *Jervis*, *Janus*, and *Hasty*, and the special service ship *Glengyle* which had landing craft and was capable herself of carrying 3,000 troops. Rear-Admiral King flew his flag in the *Phoebe* (Captain G. Grantham).

In view of the size of the losses occurring in Rawlings's Force B during the return passage on Thursday May 29th, there was immediate concern at headquarters about the *Glengyle*, then on her way to Sphakia, for if she were to be hit on her return, with 3,000 troops on board, the probable loss of life among the closely packed soldiers would be so high as to make the risk unjustified. It would be fairer to leave the soldiers to take their chance as prisoners or even to make their own attempts at escape. Wavell, after consultation with Blamey and Tedder, suggested to Cunningham that the 'Glen' ships, and also cruisers, should not be risked any further, and evacuation should be conducted by destroyers only.

Cunningham informed Admiralty of the situation, and asked if he should accept the risk of loss and damage on a scale similar to that already incurred. At the same time he made it clear that the fleet was ready and willing, so long as a ship remained, to continue the evacuation. The whole tone was in line with his remark that it takes the Navy three years to build a new ship, but 300 years to build a new tradition. Late on Thursday May 29th the Admiralty replied that the *Glengyle* should be turned back, but the remaining ships should carry on. By this time it was too late to recall the *Glengyle*, for together with the cruisers she had anchored off Sphakia beach well before midnight, using her landing craft to carry off the waiting troops from the beach, and then in turn to feed the destroyers when they closed in one at a time for their quota. The *Calcutta* and *Coventry*, which were not to be used to carry troops, meanwhile kept watch to seaward.

Finding that it was too late to stop the *Glengyle* embarkation, and every moment being precious, Cunningham ordered three destroyers, with Captain Waller in command in the *Stuart* accompanied by the *Jaguar* and *Defender*, to act as a supporting force on the return journey. This force would not embark troops, but would be available to rescue troops if any ship were lost. Cunningham informed the Admiralty of his intentions, and these were approved.

Force D had had a relatively uneventful passage to Sphakia, receiving one attack from a Ju88 that dropped a stick of bombs near the *Perth* without causing any damage. The *Perth* was carrying two assault landing craft. These together with those of the *Glengyle* effectually speeded embarkation, and there was no longer any need to use destroyers' boats as on the previous night.

There had as yet been little German pressure on the Sphakia retreat, but it must come soon. On the afternoon of Thursday May 29th, General Weston had conferred with his three brigadiers Hargest, Inglis, and Vasey, and decided that the vulnerable 'Saucer' at Askifou, ten miles from Sphakia, could be held until nightfall on Thursday by the 4th New Zealand Brigade. After dark the latter would retire towards the dispersal area near the coast. A new and final defence was to be prepared at Vitsilokoumos, two miles from Sphakia, a particularly strategic point at a narrow bend in the road. With three remaining tanks and three Bren carriers, the Royal Marine Battalion and the 19th Australian Brigade were to hold this position, while Layforce and the 5th New Zealand Brigade moved towards the dispersal area for the beach.

The intense attacks which were concentrated on Rawlings's squadron on that Black Thursday had resulted in a day of only small

German air activity on Sphakia. But this was compensated by a heavy attack on assembly lines and the embarkation beaches by sixty German aircraft at dusk.

The withdrawal towards the dispersal area of the 5th New Zealand Brigade, more than a thousand men, was carried out in good order, the men moving in single file. There had been some panic-stricken gate-crashing on the previous night, before proper controls could be imposed to ensure an orderly withdrawal. The number required for embarkation depended entirely on the capacity and number of ships that would be available. Too much flexibility could lead to congestion and vulnerability; too much control could delay assembly and arrival at point of embarkation, thus cutting down the total taken off.

The weather was clear and the wind light as the embarkation proceeded on the morning of Friday May 30th, the flat bottomed shallow draft landing craft from *Glengyle* and *Perth*, plying backwards and forwards, proving ideal for the operation. Officers from the ships had been sent on shore to explain to the troops the procedure and the vital necessity for quiet, especially in the event of the Germans dropping flares from aircraft. It was in almost total silence that the weary and footsore soldiers stumbled and limped as directed. By 03.20hrs/30, over 6,000 men had been taken off the beach. Three motor landing craft were left behind for subsequent use. King's Force D sailed for Alexandria at 03.20hrs, being joined $3\frac{1}{2}$ hours later by Waller's supporting force of the three destroyers *Stuart, Jaguar,* and *Defender*. Once again the Sphakia embarkation was to be luckier than that from Heraklion, the principal reason on this day being the welcome presence of RAF fighters giving cover to the force for most of the day. The fighters drove off twenty Ju87s and Ju88s during one attack, and in various sorties damaged enemy aircraft. Two He 111s were shot down.

The first air attack did not take place until 09.30hrs, and in this the *Perth* (Captain Sir P. W. Bowyer-Smith) received a direct hit which put her foremost boiler room out of action. A second and third attack followed but no direct hits were scored. There was no further intervention, and King brought Force D safely to Alexandria by the evening of Friday May 30th with more than 6,000 troops rescued in this the second evacuation from Sphakia. It was on this day that he was promoted Vice-Admiral.

The total brought off so far amounted to about 11,000, comprising: 700 from Sphakia in Arliss's Force C, 4,000 from Heraklion in

Rawling's Force B, and over 6,000 from Sphakia in King's Force D.

It was estimated that there were still 7,000 disciplined troops concentrated around Sphakia and on the stretch of road from the 'Saucer' to the beach, on the morning of Friday May 30th. It was also apparent that there were very many more who were now just stragglers, not under the control of any parent unit, making their way to the coast independently, raising the total to perhaps 10,000. Four destroyers, the *Napier*, *Nizam*, *Kelvin*, and *Kandahar*, forming a further Force C, again under Arliss, had left Alexandria at 09.15hrs on Friday May 30th for Sphakia. By 15.30hrs this force had been reduced to two, the *Kandahar* returning to base because of mechanical trouble, and then the *Kelvin* being detached when her speed was reduced to 20 knots by a near miss from an aircraft.

It was on this day, Friday May 30th, that two battalions of the German 100th Mountain Regiment began an attack on the Sphakia rearguard soon after sunrise. This led to some spirited fighting in which one of the British tanks was knocked out and our troops were forced to withdraw to a new holding position. Demolition was prepared and carried out by the 42nd Field Company of Royal Engineers, and withdrawals continued, before the frontal assault of the Germans who now had with them three light tanks. And so the fighting retreat continued all this day, the two British tanks being finally rendered unserviceable. Lieut Upham, VC, again distinguished himself, by leading a platoon on a long detour up the western face of the cliffs until, upon reaching the crest, they found men of the 100th Mountain Regiment below them, exposed and at their mercy.

By nightfall the rearguard had withdrawn to a position south of Vitsilokoumos, only a mile and a half from the end of the road. Here the central pass was securely held by two battalions of Australians and a battalion of the Royal Marines supported on the flanks by Layforce and New Zealanders. But the Germans had already begun a slow and difficult outflanking movement on both sides. They could not fail, and time was on their side for the British and Imperial troops lacked food and water, and almost everything else except courage and the determination to evacuate as many troops as possible in a controlled manner.

Captain Arliss arrived at Sphakia with his two destroyers at 00.30hrs on Saturday May 31st, and in 2½ hours had embarked as many as 1,510 troops, including most of the 4th New Zealand

Brigade, using the three landing craft that had been left behind the previous night, supplemented by ships' boats.

On this same night a Sunderland flying-boat arrived off Sphakia to embark Major-General Freyberg, VC, and Captain Morse, who had been ordered by Wavell and Cunningham respectively to return to Egypt. Though they faced the ignominy of defeat to the end they had both preserved a stout-hearted front to the end. Freyberg handed over command of remaining troops to General Weston.

At 06.25hrs, Force C had the welcome sight of RAF fighters who shot down in the course of the day three Ju88s and a Cant 1007. There was a heavy attack by twelve Ju88s between 08.50hrs and 09.15hrs, in which both the *Napier* and the *Nizam* were damaged by near misses, the former suffering a reduction of speed to 23 knots. The two destroyers managed between them however to shoot down a Ju88 and hit three others. They entered the harbour at Alexandria that evening without further incident, with their load of 1,510 soldiers safe.

The total so far was between 12,000 and 13,000 evacuated as follows:

Thursday May 29th: 700 from Sphakia (Arliss); 4,000 from Heraklion (Rawlings).
Friday May 30th: 6,000 from Sphakia (King).
Saturday May 31st: 1,510 from Sphakia (Arliss).

This still left a remainder, estimated at first as 3,000, and Freyberg had asked as far back as Friday May 30th that they should be taken off in the early morning of Sunday June 1st if ships could be provided. This estimate had been made in Crete after the evacuation of more than 6,000 from Sphakia by King's force on the morning of Friday May 30th, and in the belief that at least 3,000 would be embarked the next day, when in fact only two destroyers were able to arrive off Sphakia. After Arliss had left with 1,510 troops in his two destroyers on the morning of Saturday May 31st, a new estimate suggested that there were still 6,500 men to come off from Sphakia. In fact the figure must have been nearer 9,500 or 10,000. It had been a race between embarkation and the final compulsion to surrender. Each operation of passage, embarkation, and return, had lasted a day and a half, quite apart from the time expended in refuelling and replenishment at Alexandria before and after. There were just not enough ships fit for sea available to get to Sphakia in time, bearing in mind the necessarily limited hours occasioned by the risk of daylight bombing.

After consultation with Wavell on Friday May 30th, Cunningham had reluctantly agreed that there should be a further final evacuation on the morning of Sunday June 1st. It seemed at that time, owing to miscalculation of remaining troops, that this might achieve complete withdrawal. Cunningham could never forget the sight of Rawlings's battered ships returning to Alexandria; but even more in his mind was the picture of carnage on the *Orion*'s mess-decks, and the terrible casualties imposed among the crowded troops. He was very concerned about the limitations in a ship crammed with troops to an extent such that she would be seriously hindered from effective fighting.

Mr Fraser, the Prime Minister of New Zealand, was still in Alexandria, and had called on Cunningham on the afternoon of Friday May 30th to ask that further effort should be made to evacuate New Zealanders from Crete. Cunningham had earmarked the destroyers *Kimberley*, *Hotspur*, and *Jackal*, together with the fast minelayer *Abdiel*, for the final evacuation on the morning of Sunday June 1st; he was reluctant to risk any more cruisers. He now agreed however that the *Phoebe*, still on passage from Sphakia to Alexandria with King's Force D and 6,000 evacuees, should make a quick turn round after arrival and join the final evacuation force. That night, Cunningham went to meet the *Phoebe* on her return to Alexandria at 23.00hrs, and told the ship's company that the ship was to leave at 06.00hrs the next morning, Saturday May 31st, to carry out the final evacuation; he would find a relief for anybody who did not want to go. All volunteered to return, more scared of Cunningham than of the Luftwaffe, it has been said. It must be realised however that with fighter protection available the menace from the air was far less terrifying. In any case the ship's company of the *Phoebe* had by now seen enough of the sort of men who were waiting, and had heard enough of their plight to want to help at whatever cost.

As soon as the final Force D had sailed, under King in the *Phoebe*, Cunningham received a visit from Fraser, Wavell, Freyberg, and Evetts, on that Saturday May 31st. As a result of their deliberations, in spite of the conflicting reports as to the number of troops still to be taken off at Sphakia, there seems to have been general agreement that King's five ships would suffice if filled to capacity. Cunningham thereupon decided that this must be the last effort, and on that

Saturday informed the Admiralty that he had called a halt and there would be no further evacuation after that which was to take place in the early morning of Sunday June 1st. He added that even if the ships employed in this final evacuation escaped with no damage, the Mediterranean Fleet had already been reduced to two battleships, one cruiser, two anti-aircraft cruisers, one minelayer, and nine destroyers fit for service.

Owing to signalling difficulties, many hours were to pass before Weston at Sphakia learnt of the decision concerning the final evacuation. At 16.00hrs that Saturday he sent a message to say that 9,000 troops remained, and he had every hope of hanging on until the morning of Monday June 2nd. This conflicted greatly with the views expressed at the meeting with Wavell and Freyberg early on Saturday, and Cunningham therefore resolutely refused to change his mind and determined to stick to the agreed plan.

At about 20.00hrs, Wavell requested Cunningham to pass a message to Weston, the naval radio link being the only practical means of communication left. The message informed Weston of the decision that the evacuation that night would be the last, and authorised capitulation of any troops that were left behind. He himself, after turning over command to the senior remaining army officer, was to return to Egypt in a flying-boat that would be at Sphakia that night.

In the meantime the gallant rearguard sticking staunchly to their positions at Vitsilokoumos were confident of holding back the Germans, and moreover optimistic of a safe withdrawal. But, unknown to them, the limit had already been passed.

HMAS *Stuart*

HMS *Hasty* (undamaged)

HMS *Hereward* (sunk May 29th, 1941)

HMS *Havock* (damaged May 23rd, 1941)

Top: HMS *Hotspur*, which sank the *Imperial* on May 29th, 1941

Above: HMS *Nubian*, which had her stern blown off on May 26th, 1941

Above: HMS *Jackal* (escaped damage)

Above right: HMS *Kashmir* (sunk May 23rd, 1941)

Right: HMS *Kelly*, Mountbatten's flotilla leader, which was sunk on May 23rd, 1941

HMS *Kipling* returning to Alexandria with *Kelly* and *Kashmir* survivors, including Captain Lord Mountbatten, on May 24th, 1941

HMS *Kelvin* (badly damaged May 30th, 1941)

HMS *Kingston* (slightly damaged May 22nd, 1941)

HMAS *Napier* (considerably damaged May 31st, 1941)

HMAS *Nizam* with the *Napier*, completed two evacuation
operations from Sphakia. She suffered slight damage on
May 31st, 1941

The mine-laying submarine HMS *Rorqual*

CHAPTER ELEVEN

Last Journey

Vice-Admiral King, flying his flag in the cruiser *Phoebe*, in company with the fast minelayer *Abdiel*, and the three destroyers *Kimberley*, *Hotspur*, and *Jackal*, sailed from Alexandria at 06.00hrs on Saturday May 31st, for what was to be the final evacuation which, it had been initially hoped, would result in the complete withdrawal from Sphakia.

In spite of the late decision to add the *Phoebe* to Force D, it was already known that the capacity of the ships would still be too small to take off all the troops. Estimates varied, but the latest figure from Weston suggested that there were still 9,000 troops in Crete.* Less than 4,000 could be brought back by Force D, even when filled to capacity. It seemed, therefore, in view of Cunningham's determination to stick to the agreed plan, that 5,000 would have to be left in the island without food and supplies. Weston had already, on May 31st, left instructions for them to surrender after the final evacuation.

General Blamey had been perturbed at the small number of Australians evacuated so far, and had asked Cunningham for a ship to be sent to Plaka. There was however no evidence of troops having assembled there, and under the circumstances it was essential to concentrate at Sphakia all ships for the final withdrawal. Cunningham alone seemed to shoulder the tremendous responsibility of saying 'yes' or 'no', and it is greatly to his credit that he remained steadfast at a time when others might have wavered. Crete was not his only worry, for there was Malta to be concerned about, and Tobruk, and the constant procession of convoys from Italy feeding Rommel's troops in North Africa; to say nothing of the fresh crews and fine warships lying in Italian harbours. Without serviceable ships Cunningham could quickly lose the war in the Mediterranean.

Fighters of the RAF were in attendance for the last journey to Sphakia, and forced many of the German bombers to ditch their

---

* Fighting troops 4,000; mixed formations 3,500 and scattered troops 1,500 (total 9,000).

bombs prematurely. Although attacked three times during daylight hours, King's squadron remained undamaged and eventually arrived safely at Sphakia well before midnight. While ships lay in close, and began loading from the motor landing craft and ships' boats, *Hotspur* acted as a submarine screen and guard ship for prowling enemy motor-boats. But not a single unit of the Italian Navy ventured near on that quiet night, though Sphakia was less than 400 miles from Taranto.

Rearguard positions had been firmly held right up to dark, by the 19th Australian Brigade, a few light gun carriers of the 3rd Hussars, the Royal Marine Battalion, and Layforce. The wide flanking attempts on both sides by the Germans had not yet advanced sufficiently to interfere with withdrawal. The order of final embarkation arranged by Weston gave priority to those troops who had done so much fighting west of Canea and latterly in the rearguard: the 5th New Zealand Brigade (about 1,100) were to go first, then the remainder of the 4th New Zealand Brigade (200), the 19th Australian Brigade (1,250), Layforce (500), and the Royal Marine Battalion (550). In accordance with Weston's orders, strong guards were posted at the beach approaches in order to secure this priority for the organised formations, and to prevent any rush from the many stragglers. Brigadier Hargest of the 5th New Zealand Brigade was determined that his men should withdraw in an orderly manner, clean shaven and properly armed. Any man without a rifle was to be treated as a straggler. As it grew dark, the Brigade closed up and descended the hill in utter silence, at a slow pace so that no straggler could break in. Every man had a weapon, and each wore a helmet, haversack, and bayonet. There was a faint light from the moon at first quarter, and murmurs of admiration from the stragglers in the shadows, waiting and hoping (perhaps despairingly) for their turn. Many of those who failed to escape this time survived the war, and many of those who were evacuated this night, later lost their lives in Egypt. Such are the fortunes of war.

The embarkation began in a smooth manner and in accordance with schedule, but as it continued it was realised that the numbers of stragglers, deserters, and refugees were growing, and that many had evaded pickets and been taken on board, some limping along with the wounded men or wearing faked bandages. The information that this was the last evacuation spread rapidly, and hundreds of un-authorised men began to descend the narrow path to the beach, causing a blockage. In view of the congestion men sat on the path.

The Australians who had held the final position on the escarpment, now spent and weary, found their way blocked when it came to their turn to descend. Of the 500 in the 2/7th Australian Battalion only sixteen succeeded in getting through to the boats. The remainder arrived on the beach after ships' boats had been hoisted and the landing craft abandoned, in time to hear the weighing of the ships' anchors. Others also left behind with them were the Commandos who had put up such a gallant stand at Babali Khani, and the Royal Marines who had formed the rearguard. Fortune does not always favour the brave.

Some excuse has been made for the rabble of men who broke formation, and it is said that many of them had realised that in the ships that had left on previous nights there had been room for more troops. There is no doubt that the absence of a suitable assembly area near to the small beach presented great difficulties and led to an inflexibility of control which at times considerably reduced the speed of evacuation. To balance the account of stragglers and gate-crashing are the stories of detachments marching with equipment in perfect order, groups waiting their turn with stoic discipline and patience, and of some who declined a place in a boat in order to take rations back to their friends who had fallen by the wayside.

Weston's final hours at Sphakia on Saturday May 31st, and in the early morning of Sunday June 1st, before he took off in a flying-boat for Alexandria as ordered, were very much occupied not only with concern for the progress of the evacuation but in turning over instructions to 'the Senior Officer left on the island'. The radio link was already becoming sporadic in performance, and although a personal message to Weston from Wavell was received, there seems to have been no final authorisation for surrender from the Middle East command. The message indicated that confusion remained over numbers still to be withdrawn. It said:

'You know the heroic effort the Navy has made. I hope you will be able to get away most of those who remain, but this is the last night the Navy can come. Please tell those that have to be left that the fight put up against such odds has won the admiration of us all and every effort to bring them back is being made. General Freyberg has told me how magnificently your Marines have fought and of your own grand work. I have heard also of the heroic fighting of young Greek soldiers. I send you my grateful thanks.'

There was now no alternative to surrender, although pockets of resistance and individual enterprises were certain to continue, limited only by shortage of food. Weston's instructions, handed over to a Lieut-Colonel of the Commandos, explained that as preference in the final evacuation had been given to fighting troops, many of the soldiers left behind would be unable to offer organised resistance. In view of this, combined with the absence of rations, no radio, and no further evacuation, contact was to be made with the enemy to arrange capitulation.

On arrival by flying-boat in Alexandria, Weston immediately signalled Middle East Command requesting that food be dropped by air in a suitable area not too far from the hungry and weary soldiers left behind in Crete. This was done. Not all of the 5,000 remaining troops became prisoners of war, as we shall see when following their exploits later in this chapter.

Having embarked nearly 4,000 troops, King sailed from Sphakia at 03.00hrs on Sunday June 1st for Alexandria. A little later on this morning, the relatively slow anti-aircraft cruisers *Calcutta* (Captain D. M. Lees) and *Coventry* (Captain W. P. Carne), that had accompanied King's Force D two days earlier, sailed from Alexandria to rendezvous with King to give substantial support to his anti-aircraft defence for the final part of the journey to Alexandria. Ironically, the cruisers themselves were attacked when still only eighty-five miles from Alexandria at 09.00hrs. The *Coventry* sighted at that moment on her radar screen enemy aircraft approaching from the northward. Within twenty minutes two Ju88s dived from the direction of the sun. A stick of bombs from the first aircraft narrowly missed the *Coventry*. That from the second aircraft was more accurate: two bombs hit the *Calcutta*. She settled fast and sank in a matter of minutes. If it was hazardous for two ships, it was imperative for the *Coventry*, now alone, to return to harbour. She succeeded in rescuing 23 officers and 232 men, and immediately set course for Alexandria. King's squadron on the other hand, still only halfway home, with 180 miles farther to go, continued without any serious trouble, and entered harbour at Alexandria with her 4,000 troops at 17.00hrs that afternoon.

The loss of the little *Calcutta* was yet a further serious blow to

Cunningham, and was greatly felt. He himself had commanded her as Flag Captain to Admiral Sir Walter Cowan in the West Indies 1926–28. Since joining the Mediterranean Fleet in September 1940 she had been in action practically every time she had been at sea, and had a good record of safely escorted convoys. In the last twelve days Cunningham had lost, either sunk or put out of action, 25 ships. Even more tragic was the loss of nearly 2,000 officers and men killed. Such heavy losses could be expected and tolerated only, say, in a major fleet action in which similar or greater losses were inflicted on the enemy. 'We are short of air power' had been the Navy's cry, and Cunningham had repeatedly asked for help in the air. Fighting against the strength of the Luftwaffe without long-range fighters or the support of aircraft carriers had exacted its tragic toll. A year or two were to pass before the situation was rectified.

But on the credit side was the rescue of more than 16,000 Allied troops, and the virtual annihilation of the cream of German paratroopers. (*See Appendices.*) Perhaps more important was the delay which had been imposed on Hitler's coming assault on Russia.

Early on Sunday June 1st Cunningham received a signal from the First Sea Lord saying that if there was any reasonable chance of embarking any substantial formed body of men in the early hours of Monday the attempt should be made. Cunningham replied informing him of Weston's instructions to the hungry and exhausted men to capitulate. In the circumstances no further ships would be sent.

At Sphakia on Sunday June 1st it was fine with a morning mist, and all seemed quiet. Many of the men did not realise that the last evacuation had indeed taken place, and when informed they reacted with surprise, anger, and in some cases despair. Others went in search of food and weapons, and moved off to the eastward along the coast. Some began to fraternise with Germans who had come down the escarpment. A few looked at the abandoned landing craft and boats. At about 08.45hrs four German dive bombers and four fighters flew along the shore killing victor and defeated alike. The surrender had caught them unprepared, and this was a demonstration of mastery calculated to deter resistance to the rounding up which would follow.

Of those determined to avoid surrender, Major R. Garrett of the Royal Marines was one of the first off the mark. Informing his men that he was not staying behind to be taken prisoner, he quickly acquired one of the abandoned landing craft. This was not only seaworthy, but still laden with provisions. With the help of two Australians, he got the engine going, warped the lighter inshore, and was soon joined by 134 other ranks consisting of Royal Marines, Commandos, Australians, and New Zealanders. A heaven-sent mist was drifting in, and this concealed their combined efforts of collecting arms, petrol, water, and rations. By 09.00hrs they had cast off and were making for the island of Gaudopula, roughly twenty miles to the southward. Here they secured in a cave while preparations were made for a long journey, the navigation of which would be performed by the help of a small scale atlas and a magnetic compass: their objective was Tobruk, 180 miles due south, still in British hands though almost surrounded by Rommel's troops. The only access for the Allies was by sea, and Garrett was determined to exploit to the full what still remained of British sea power. After replenishing further with water he made a complete survey of resources, ensured that everybody would have one good meal before departure, and at 21.30hrs on that Sunday June 1st set course for Tobruk. It should be realised that the craft was designed to accommodate only 100 men for a few hours. During the first night there was trouble with the steering gear and engine, and the motion of the sea caused severe seasickness while the craft was stopped for examination and repairs. Undeterred, Garrett made a rough sail out of a canvas cover, and this steadied the craft until the engine was restarted. But by 18.00hrs on Monday June 2nd the petrol was exhausted, and the craft again wallowed slowly on under the strip of canvas. By Tuesday rations had been reduced to a sixth of a pint of water, a cube of bully-beef, and half a biscuit. The water situation was however improved by improvising a distilling plant using sea-water, two petrol cans, and diesel oil as a heating agent.

Prospects of survival with such slow progress were diminishing, and it was therefore decided to increase sail area by making two square-sails, the big one from six blankets sewn together and set forward above the square-nosed bow, and the smaller one aft at the control position. This worked well except for a tendency for the craft to yaw either side of the desired course, and a refusal to answer the helm. This could be remedied only by parties of men plunging over the bows in relays, and swimming with concerted force to push the boat in the desired direction.

Though exhausted and almost starving, these gallant determined men spared no effort to achieve their aim. A small canoe was devised, and a raft was built from oil drums and deck-boards: they might come in handy, just as the poles, ropes, and blankets had. But exposure and weariness combined with deprivation was too much for two men, who died on Sunday June 8th, a week after the beginning of their desperate journey. On the evening of the same day, not long before sunset, land sighted. Eight hours later the landing craft was run on to a sandy beach. Various parties were sent ashore to explore with discretion, and find water.

Their luck was in. Although they had missed Tobruk by 100 miles, their landfall was to the eastward of that isolated and besieged town. They were now in Allied-held territory, only seventeen miles from Sidi Barrani. At the latter was the headquarters of the 1st Anti-Aircraft Regiment. The following morning, Tuesday June 10th, Major Garrett marched his gallant force across the desert to the coastal road where lorries awaited them. They were home and dry (or almost); and still unbeaten. Crete is a tragic tale in our history, but defeat is ameliorated by stories of derring-do which act as an inspiration and tonic.

Garrett's was only one of a number of determined attempts made by troops who had been left behind in Crete. There were 700 or more men who in various small parties escaped to Africa, arriving on the coast as late as September either in boats or in landing craft. The submarine *Thrasher*, while engaged on special duties on July 28th, took off 78 men (including twelve Greeks) who had been in hiding, and the submarine *Torbay* 120 men, on August 19th.

When Rawlings had evacuated the Heraklion garrison so successfully on the morning of May 29th, a platoon of the Black Watch had had to be left behind at Knossos, as there was no means of communication which could reach them in time. In due course this party extricated itself and moved southward to Ay Dheka where it joined a marooned company of the Argyll and Sutherland Highlanders. Together they covered the remaining ten miles to Tymbaki, and here they were joined by 100 Australians who had managed to break through the perimeter round Retimo after the surrender. There were no Germans in the vicinity, and rations were dropped by a RAF Blenheim on June 1st. The following day a party of 11 officers and 66 men succeeded in making a disused landing craft serviceable, and sailed for Africa. But they were unlucky to be sighted the next morning by an Italian submarine. The officers were taken off, and the rest allowed to proceed on a relatively straightforward passage that ended, fortunately for them, at Mersa Matruh in Egypt, about 100 miles east of Sidi Barrani. Such escapes proved to be great morale builders.

Those men who were unable to get away from Crete had to take to the hills, where they were sheltered by Cretans, for the Germans soon had control of the southern beaches and removed all large boats. Aircraft also patrolled the coast to frustrate further escapes. The Germans treated their captives with reasonable humanity, but became impatient at the knowledge that armed British troops were at large in the mountains, assisting Cretan guerillas. These were threatened with dire punishment if they failed to surrender. Nevertheless there were still 500 soldiers at large as late as the close of 1941.

Losses on both sides in this tragic twelve-days' battle for Crete were very great and are given in detail in the Appendix. The results of the struggle are examined in the next and final chapter of the narrative.

Cunningham's despatch after the battle brings out well the tragedy of the losses suffered by the Navy in supporting and rescuing the Army, and pays due tribute to the officers and men who were involved. He writes:

'It is not easy to convey how heavy was the strain that men and ships sustained. Apart from the cumulative effect of prolonged sea-going over extended periods it has to be remembered that in this last instance ships' companies had none of the inspiration of battle with the enemy to bear them up. Instead they had the unceasing anxiety of the task of trying to bring away in safety, thousands of their own countrymen, many of whom were in an exhausted and dispirited condition, in ships necessarily so over-crowded that even when there was opportunity to relax, conditions made this impossible. They had started the evacuation already over-tired, and they had to carry it through under conditions of savage air attacks such as had only recently caused grievous losses in the fleet.

There is rightly little credit or glory to be expected in these operations of retreat, but I feel that the spirit of tenacity shown by those who took part should not go unrecorded.

More than once I felt that the stage had been reached when no more could be asked of officers and men, physically and mentally exhausted by their efforts and by the events of these fateful days. It is perhaps even now not realised how nearly the breaking point was reached, but that these men struggled through is the measure of their achievement, and I trust that it will not lightly be forgotten.'

On conclusion of the final evacuation Cunningham received a personal message from General Sir Archibald Wavell which was promulgated to the fleet:

'I send to you and all under your command the deepest admiration and gratitude of the Army in the Middle East for the magnificent work of the Royal Navy in bringing the troops back from Crete. The skill and self-sacrifice with which the difficult and dangerous operation was carried out will never be forgotten, and will form another strong link between our two services. Our thanks to all and sympathy for your losses.'

On the same day Tedder sent the following message:

'May I express on behalf of myself and the Royal Air Force, Middle East, our admiration of the way in which the Royal Navy has once again succeeded in doing what seemed almost impossible.'

I should like to quote two extracts of letters, written, shortly after the evacuation, by Major Ian Manson, 23 Battalion, 5 NZ Brigade, 2/NZEF on July 27th, 1941:

'Most of us lost all our personal belongings and came out (of Greece) with what we stood up in.

During the first week on Crete we quite recovered and then started to prepare for the defence of the island. The battle lasted for 12 days and was a most unhappy experience. We had food when we could get it, but nothing hot, not even a hot cup of tea for the 12 days. The odds were against us from the start, one can't fight aeroplanes with bayonets. The German dive bombing and machine-gunning from the air was terrific. The evacuation involved a journey over steep mountainous country of about 50 miles on foot, marching by night and fighting rearguard actions by day. I had a thrilling trip from Crete to Alexandria on board a destroyer* doing 35 knots. The ship shook from stem to stern.'

* HMS *Nizam* Saturday May 31st

After a period of sickness in and out of hospital, Major Manson writes:

'We hope that the next time we are in action that there will be no withdrawal. New Zealand will never be able to thank the Royal Navy for its work at great cost of men and ships, in evacuating us from Greece and Crete.'

Here are words of which the Royal Navy might well be proud. It would take years to recover from those terrible losses of men and ships, but a tradition of centuries had been maintained.

CHAPTER TWELVE

Conclusion

Summary of the Battle

The loss of Crete after a resistance of only a few days caused quite a sensation, and added much to the growing reputation of German invincibility. There were prospects of more assaults, perhaps on Cyprus or in Syria or Iraq. German prestige was so high that when their blitzkrieg on Russia began, three weeks after Crete, it was believed that there would be little to stop them; Russia might collapse in a matter of weeks.

Not only had Crete been lost to the Allies, but a very heavy price had been paid in defending it. The Mediterranean Fleet had lost, in addition to 2,000 officers and men killed, three cruisers, the *Gloucester*, *Fiji*, and *Calcutta*, and six destroyers, *Juno*, *Greyhound*, *Kashmir*, *Kelly*, *Imperial*, and *Hereward*; all sunk. Moreover, the only aircraft carrier in the Eastern Mediterranean, the *Formidable*, had been put out of action for months, together with the battleships *Warspite* and *Barham*, the cruisers *Ajax*, *Orion*, *Dido*, and *Perth*, and the destroyers *Kelvin* and *Nubian*. Also damaged and requiring repairs that might take weeks to complete were the cruisers *Naiad* and *Carlisle*, and destroyers *Napier*, *Ilex*, *Havock*, *Kingston*, and *Nizam*. The Italian fleet had made no appearance in strength, and suffered no losses. Cunningham's surviving two battleships and three cruisers were therefore well outnumbered now by their four battleships and eleven cruisers.

The defending army in Crete, including last minute reinforcements, amounted to about 32,000. Of these, in rough figures, 1,800 had been killed, 12,000 taken prisoner, and 17,000 evacuated; about 1,000 escaped after the evacuation of the island.

The RAF in the Middle East had suffered severely from shortages and the absence of suitably placed permanent bases. With only a limited number of aircraft, they had been unable to provide support of the size that was forthcoming in following years; nevertheless they lost 23 bombers and 23 fighters. Gallant sorties were made with

Marylands, Blenheims, Wellingtons, and Hurricanes, flying from North Africa, the fighters being forced to reduce their ammunition load in order to fit extra fuel tanks to enable them to cover the great distances and spend some time over the operational area. Particulars of aircraft are given in Appendix I (B).

There is disagreement on the figures concerning German losses. Certainly the slaughter was very heavy in the first few days, and particularly so in the assault at Heraklion. The Germans admit to 4,000 killed and missing, but it is believed that the figure could hardly be less than 5,000, and may have been very much higher when account is taken of those who were dropped into the sea, and those who died in the abortive sea expeditions. General Freyberg estimated at the time that the losses (killed and wounded) were 17,000, including 6,000 drowned. These losses were more particularly severe since they involved specially trained air troops.

The Lutwaffe lost 200 fighters, bombers, and reconnaissance and transport planes in the operation. These were large numbers at that period of the war.

Lessons

A surprising feature about the Mediterranean is the relative lack of interest displayed towards it after the Abyssinian crisis, not only by Germany, but also by Britain who neglected especially the matter of air power. By the time our shortages in that sea were beginning to be realised we were fighting for our existence and so obsessed with the Battle of Britain that little could be spared for the Mediterranean. The shortages were well realised by Cunningham as soon as France collapsed and Italy entered the war, but it required a tragedy such as Crete to bring home fully to Britain the desperate need for aircraft and suitably based airfields in the Eastern Mediterranean.

It was perhaps fortunate for Britain that Hitler tended to regard the Mediterranean as an Italian sphere of interest, in spite of Admiral Raeder's attempt to persuade him to exploit that sea to the full. It was not until January 1941 that Fliegerkorps X arrived in Sicily. The future of Malta then became precarious, but within four months the Germans turned to Crete. By the time Crete had fallen, not only had Fliegerkorps X suffered heavy losses, though light compared with the crippling losses suffered by Fliegerkorps VIII and Fliegerkorps XI, but commitments further afield had become very pressing. Malta was thus granted a further lease of life. History is full of the failures that attended commanders who neglected the importance of the Mediterranean.

After the fall of Crete, Wavell issued a signal (see Appendix G) enumerating the lessons produced by an inter-services committee. They all sound so obvious, but it should be remembered that this was the first full-scale airborne assault against a defended position. Although such an assault on this scale was never repeated by the Germans because of the huge losses, General Student was to use his airborne troops again with great skill but under very different circumstances, at Arnhem in 1944.

With regard to naval operations, the principal lesson which emerged was one already fully recognised by Cunningham, namely that ships cannot operate close to enemy airfields unless given adequate and timely fighter support. Without this they were bound to suffer heavy losses. The already accepted principle of concentration of ships' anti-aircraft fire had been fully borne out in the battle.

The records of enemy air attacks upon British warships reveal the tremendous weight of offensive brought to bear, particularly within thirty miles of air bases. What those ships were able to accomplish under the circumstances is astonishing and admirable.

For the first time in history, a highly strategic island had been captured from the air. And this in spite of the fact that the defenders were expecting the attack almost to the hour, and enjoyed command of the sea. There was much to be learnt on both sides, not the least being the extremely high cost in men and aircraft of an airborne assault even when the aggressor dominated the air.

Previous German airborne assaults had taken place in Holland and Belgium against an unprepared foe, and casualties had been relatively light. Consolidation by ground troops had followed with comparative ease. But at Crete the defenders were ready, and treated the assailant mercilessly. Moreover the Royal Navy had performed its task of preventing any seaborne support, though at a cost which imperilled the maintenance of sea power in the Eastern Mediterranean. Britain had been in occupation of Crete for more than six months. With airfields such as Maleme, a garrison of some 30,000, prepared defence positions, and local command of the sea, Crete appeared to be safe. Why then, it may be asked, was Germany able to take it in a matter of days? Why were the defenders unable, after such a lengthy occupation, to frustrate the 'softening-up' which preceded the final assault?

Was this a lost opportunity?

It would be out of place in a book dealing mainly with the naval aspect, to criticise the purely military defence of the island, particularly in view of the many deeds of gallantry and the determined stand made by the defending troops which culminated in a courageous withdrawal fraught with uncertainty and insoluble problems. There are many who deplore the absence of a speedy and effective counter-attack on the very first night of the assault, which they argue would have positively denied Maleme airfield to the Germans. Others point to the successful repulses at Heraklion and Retimo. There are many accounts of lost opportunities. But the fact remains that the dominating feature of the battle lay in the almost unchallenged command of the air possessed by the aggressor. The defenders were powerless to do much about this, except perhaps in the matter of making Maleme airfield unusable. The material effect of the 'softening-up' phase was in itself substantial, leading as it did to the withdrawal of British aircraft from the island before the assault. The unceasing bombing and strafing during the assault phase almost neutralised the defence, but by far the most important feature of these aircraft attacks, almost completely unopposed in the last few days of the assault, was the gradual weakening of confidence and morale. Another advantageous feature of supremacy in the air was its effect on intelligence. Forced to take cover under the incessant attacks from the air, the defenders were denied the means of assessing the movement of troops, and their commanders were unable to get an overall picture of the disposition of either their own or the enemy troops. This grave defect was augmented by poor communication inherent in the topography and general conditions prevailing. It must also be remembered that many of the defending troops had been hurriedly evacuated from Greece only three weeks before the assault began; and General Freyberg had taken over command as recently as April 30th, the seventh commander in six months. As in aircraft and tanks, there was a severe shortage of transport, guns, ammunition, and rations.

Why were there insufficient airfields in Crete after nearly seven months of occupation? The reason for this must rest in the priority given to other pressing requirements in the Mediterranean. Immediately upon Mussolini's invasion of Greece in October 1940, Britain had occupied Crete, and the Greeks had withdrawn their troops from the island to the mainland of Greece. Britain's chief need in the island was the harbour and small naval base at Suda Bay. The Royal Navy installed harbour defences and adapted Maleme as an air station from which both fighters and bombers could operate in the event of bombardment from the sea or air-raids from the Dodecanese Islands. It was not thought likely either by the Greeks or by the British that Italy would attempt to capture Crete. At that time Germany had shown little interest in the Mediterranean, and it was not until January 1941 that the Luftwaffe changed the whole outlook in the Mediterranean with the arrival of Fliegerkorps X in Sicily. Nor was it until April 1941, after the Yugoslav Government had aligned itself with Germany, that it became apparent that the way was now open for the Germans to push through to the Mediterranean and the Aegean Sea, bringing with them their superiority in the air. Because of Britain's desperate shortages and considerable commitments abroad as well as at home, Cunningham's and Tedder's appeals for more aircraft in the Mediterranean appeared to remain unheeded. Temporary priority had been allocated in March 1941 for 'Operation Lustre', the transport of British forces to Greece. But in little over a month all equipment and airfields in Greece had to be hurriedly abandoned, and the troops evacuated by the Royal Navy to Egypt and Crete.

British success or failure in the Western Desert depended greatly upon the extent to which Italian sea communications could be interrupted by the Royal Navy and the RAF, and this simple fact emphasised the value of Malta (as opposed to Crete, say), and the necessity of maintaining as many aircraft and ships there as possible. This provision strengthened in return the possibility of British advances in North Africa and the acquisition of airfields strategically placed to support both Cunningham's ships and Malta. It also meant that other places such as Crete might have to go without. It is ironically sad that the 238 tanks and 43 crated Hurricanes safely brought through the Mediterranean in the *Tiger* convoy to arrive at Alexandria on May 12th could not be used in the defence of Crete.

The naval and army Commanders-in-Chief had never ceased to emphasise the importance of the air aspect in their operations, and were critical of the limitations in the support given by the Middle East Air Command. Cunningham had had great value from his own aircraft carriers while they lasted, and appreciated particularly having them under his own control in the all-important matter of reconnaissance, search, bomber strikes, and fighter defence for the fleet wherever it went. In view of the great shortage of carriers (to be rectified later by the building of scores of escort carriers for Britain, in the United States), Cunningham made repeated requests for RAF aircraft to be placed under his control, especially in the matter of reconnaissance aircraft and long-range fighters. This had been consistently refused by the RAF, but long after Crete, October 20th, 1941, an RAF Naval Co-operation Group was formed under the command of an Air Commodore to work with the Naval Commander-in-Chief. This was an improvement, but in the initial stage suffered from an all-round shortage of aircraft.

Under the circumstances, in view of the general shortage of 'air' and lack of permanent airfields in May 1941, it seems unlikely that British and Imperial forces could for long prevent the Germans, with their overwhelming air superiority, from occupying Crete. The fact that they resisted for so long, extracting a very heavy toll on Germany's special airborne troops and aircraft, speaks well for the determination of their leaders and the gallantry and stamina of the defenders in the face of shortage and deprivation. If, then, defeat was inevitable, the question arises as to whether the island should have been yielded without a struggle, thus saving many lives and the heavy losses in ships.

Was Resistance worth the Price?

In spite of their overwhelming air superiority the Germans very nearly failed, and it was not until they had gained control of the airfield at Maleme on the second day that there was any glimpse of success. They threw in everything available, regardless of loss of life or cost, with the result that Fliegerkorps XI, the corps of parachute and airborne troops, were almost wiped out as a unit, together with all their transport planes, gliders, and equipment. It was their commander, General Kurt Student, whose idea it was that Crete could be taken by airborne assault, and it was only on the understanding that the operation would be speedily accomplished that Hitler gave his approval, for he required the airborne troops for his forthcoming attack on Russia. Certain units of Fliegerkorps X had been transferred from Sicily to Greece, and offensive support was also to be given by Fliegerkorps VIII, with over 700 reconnaissance, bomber, and fighter aircraft. In overall command of the attack was General Alexander Löhr.

It is pertinent to note that although the Germans had tended to regard the Mediterranean as an Italian sphere of influence until Mussolini invaded Greece, it was with speed and alacrity that they set about establishing local air superiority once Hitler had decided to intervene. The speed and efficiency with which air strength was established in Greece, the Aegean Sea, and the Dodecanese Islands, are in marked contrast with British efforts to establish an air defence in Crete. The surge of pacifism in Britain, and reliance on the League of Nations in the 'thirties', at a time when Germany was rearming and preparing for a war which they themselves would initiate, must be the excuse.

Even though the presence of the Royal Navy had frustrated the transport of German seaborne forces to Crete on a large scale, and had provided transport and replenishment for the defenders of Crete, it is obvious that this could not continue indefinitely in the absence of any reliable defence in the air.

Why then was it necessary to put up a determined struggle for the retention of an island whose doom sooner or later could generally be foreshadowed? The reason can be seen in the results. The virtual destruction of Fliegerkorps XI practically ensured that the Germans would no longer be able to support the rising Vichy forces in Syria or give much needed help to the armed rising in Iraq. Failure of Germany to interfere here was of great concern to Turkey, who might easily have been swayed from neutrality to throw in her lot with Germany just as Yugoslavia had. This would have been all the more likely had Britain given up Crete without a struggle, thereby relinquishing much of her influence in the Middle East.

There are those who still think that the British missed a great opportunity in not doing more to save Crete. Its retention would have lessened the difficulties of the fleet in supplying Malta, which were soon to arise owing to the presence of enemy aircraft in both Crete and Cyrenaica flanking 'bomb alley', the shipping route between Alexandria and Malta.

Cunningham says:*

'Looking back I sometimes wonder whether the loss of the island was really such a serious matter it seemed at the time. Had we defeated the German attack and held the island the problem of its maintenance and supply would have been extraordinarily difficult. We should undoubtedly have required a large garrison,

* *A Sailor's Odyssey*, p. 391

and though it is true that the defence could primarily have been entrusted to the Greeks, the drain on our slender resources of arms, ammunition, and equipment available in the Mediterranean would have been heavy. Moreover as has already been said, all the ports available for landing supplies were on the north coast within easy reach of enemy airfields. Though it is hardly to be expected that the Luftwaffe could maintain the same scale of attack, for it was obviously massed for the special operation of capturing the island, it is certain that the ports on the north coast could never have been used except at night.

The Royal Air Force would also have had to be maintained in considerable strength in Crete. This would have involved the construction of new airfields. When one considers all the extra equipment and supplies necessary for the RAF, to say nothing of maintaining the troops, it is difficult to see how the necessary masses of stores could have been landed on the limited beaches on the south coast of Crete, and have been transported over the mountains to where they were needed.

On the other hand, it is not to be denied that the retention of Crete would probably have done away with much of the difficulty of supplying Malta during the critical phases that were soon to come upon us. It was the German air force in Crete on the flank of our convoy route to Malta that made the maintenance of that island from the east so costly and hazardous.'

Cunningham continues with a reference to the serious effect on Germany's Balkan campaign which was caused by Britain's struggle and delaying action, first in Greece and then in Crete. Germany had begun her march through Yugoslavia and Greece on April 6th, 1941, and this campaign involved twenty-seven divisions including seven Panzer divisions (about a third of the total Panzer strength of the German army). Her detention and tremendous losses in Crete not only frustrated Hitler's designs on Syria and Iraq but seriously delayed his attack upon Russia. Cunningham continues:

'The German army reached the outskirts of Moscow in October 1941, by which time the early frost had begun to interfere with its movements. Its arrival in front of Moscow 5 weeks earlier would probably have led to the capture of that city, the importance of which it is difficult to exaggerate.

Our defence of Crete, therefore, may have served its purpose in the overall pattern of the war.'

In conclusion then, thirty-two years after the event, it is difficult to see how the outcome of the battle could have been very different. It was a losing battle fought with grim determination from the start, but with the odds against success too high, because of the enemy's domination in the air. Nevertheless that stouthearted defence was necessary and gallantly performed. It gave the Germans much to think about, for they never again attempted an airborne assault on this scale. Those many lives so gallantly given in the Allied cause were not given in vain.

Appendices

Senior Officers

Commander-in-Chief Mediterranean:
Admiral Sir Andrew B. Cunningham, GCB, DSO (HQ ashore at Alexandria)
Commander-in-Chief Middle East:
General Sir Archibald Wavell, KCB, CMG, MC (HQ at Cairo)
Air Officer Commanding-in Chief:
Air Chief Marshal Sir Arthur Longmore (until May 31st, 1941)
Air-Marshall A. W. Tedder (from June 1st, 1941)
Commander of British and Imperial Forces in Crete:
Major-General B. C. Freyberg, VC, CB, CMG, DSO (HQ at Canea)
Maleme Sector Commander:
Brigadier E. Puttick, DSO
Commanding 4th and 5th New Zealand Brigades and three Greek Battalions
Suda Sector Commander:
Major-General E. C. Weston, RM
Commanding 16th and 17th Infantry Brigades and two Greek Battalions
Retimo Sector Commander:
Brigadier G. A. Vasey, DSO
Commanding 19th Australian Brigade and three Greek Battalions
Heraklion Sector Commander:
Brigadier B. H. Chappel, MC, TD
Commanding original British Garrison
NOIC Suda Bay:
Captain J. A. V. Morse, DSO, RN
NOIC Heraklion:
Captain M. H. S. MacDonald, RN
Naval Force Commanders:
Vice-Admiral H. D. Pridham-Wippell, KCB, CVO
Rear-Admiral E. L. S. King, CB, MVO
Rear-Admiral H. B. Rawlings, OBE

Rear-Admiral I. G. Glennie
Captain H. A. Rowley, RN
Captain E. D. B. McCarthy, RN
Captain P. J. Mack, DSO, RN
Captain S. H. T. Arliss, RN
Flag Officer Aircraft Carriers:
Rear-Admiral D. W. Boyd, CBE, DSC
Captains of HM Ships:
See Appendix B: List of Warships
Commander of the German Assault:
General Alexander Löhr
Commander of the Airborne Corps (Fliegerkorps XI):
General Kurt Student

Warships at Crete

(A) BATTLESHIPS: Queen Elizabeth class
Queen Elizabeth: Captain C. B. Barry, DSO
32,700 tons, 24 knots, eight 15-inch, twenty 4.5-inch
Completed at Portsmouth 1913; reconstructed and modernised between the wars; scrapped 1948

Warspite: Captain D. B. Fisher, CBE
30,600 tons, 24 knots, eight 15-inch, eight 6-inch
Completed at Devonport 1913; reconstructed and modernised between the wars; wrecked 1947

Barham: Captain G. C. Cooke
31,000 tons, $22\frac{1}{2}$ knots, eight 15-inch, twelve 6-inch
Completed at Clydebank 1914; torpedoed and sunk November 1941 by U331, with the loss of the captain and 861 officers and men

Valiant: Captain C. E. Morgan, DSO
32,700 tons, 24 knots, eight 15-inch, twenty 4.5-inch
Completed at Fairfield 1914; reconstructed and modernised at outbreak of war; scrapped 1948

Displacement and main armament as above

ADDITIONAL ARMAMENT: sixteen to thirty-two 2 pdr mountings, several 20mm, and later 40mm multiple mountings; float-plane and catapult fitted above X turret

PROPULSION: 4-shaft geared turbines SHP 80,000=24 knots; except *Barham* 4-shaft turbines SHP 75,000=22½ knots

COMPLEMENT: 1,200

PROTECTION: main belt 4-inch (ends) 13-inch (amid.), deck 1¼ inch (ends) 4-inch (amid.), except *Queen Elizabeth* and *Valiant* deck 4–7 inches

turrets 5–13 inches

conning tower 11 inches

DIMENSIONS: length 640 feet (overall), beam 104 feet (outside bulges), draught 31 feet (*Queen Elizabeth* and *Valiant* 33 feet)

RADAR: type 279 (*Queen Elizabeth* and *Valiant* only)

(B) AIRCRAFT CARRIERS: Illustrious class (single hangar; armoured deck)

Formidable: Flagship of Rear-Admiral (Air)

Rear-Admiral D. W. Boyd, CBE, DSC

Captain A. W. LaT. Bisset

23,000 tons, 30.5 knots, sixteen 4.5-inch

Completed and commissioned at Belfast November 1940; severely damaged at Crete May 26th, 1941, but repaired in USA; scrapped at Inverkeithing 1953

Displacement and main armament as above

ADDITIONAL ARMAMENT: six multiple (8 barrel) 2 pdr mountings, ie 48 barrels, and eight 20mm

PROPULSION: 3-shaft geared turbines, SHP 110,000=30.5 knots

COMPLEMENT: 1,400

PROTECTION: main belt 4½ inches, hangar side 4½ inches, flight deck 2½–3 inches

DIMENSIONS: length 754 feet (overall), beam 96 feet, draught 24 feet

RADAR: type 279

(C) AIRCRAFT SQUADRONS AND C.O.s IN HMS FORMIDABLE

No 803, Lieutenant K. M. Bruen, DSC ⎫
No 806, Lieut-Cdr C. L. G. Evans, DSO, DSC ⎬ 12 Fulmar (fighters)
No 826, Lieut-Cdr W. H. G. Saunt, DSO ⎭ 6 Albacores (TSR)

No 829, Lieutenant W. B. Whitworth, DSC   4 Albacores (TSR)
(*See Appendix I (B) for aircraft performance details*)

(D) CRUISERS: Southampton, Fiji, Leander, Dido, Capetown, and Ceres classes

(1) SOUTHAMPTON CLASS
Gloucester: Captain H. A. Rowley
9,600 tons, $32\frac{1}{2}$ knots, twelve 6-inch
Completed at Devonport 1937, lost at Crete May 22nd, 1941
ADDITIONAL ARMAMENT: eight 4-inch AA, eight 2 pdr, eight 20mm, six 21-inch torpedo tubes, three float-planes
PROPULSION: 4-shaft geared turbines SHP 82,500 = $32\frac{1}{2}$ knots
COMPLEMENT: 700
PROTECTION: main belt 4 inches, deck 2 inches, turrets 2 inches, conning tower 4 inches
DIMENSIONS: length 592 feet (overall), beam 62 feet, draught $17\frac{1}{2}$ feet
RADAR: nil

(2) FIJI CLASS
Fiji: Captain P. B. R. W. William-Powlett
8,000 tons, 33 knots, twelve 6-inch
Completed at Clydebank 1939; lost at Crete May 22nd, 1941
ADDITIONAL ARMAMENT: eight 4-inch AA, nine 2 pdr AA, eight 0.5-inch, six 21-inch torpedo tubes, three float-planes
PROPULSION: 4-shaft geared turbines SHP 72,500 = 33 knots
COMPLEMENT: 730
PROTECTION: main belt $3\frac{1}{4}$ inches, deck 2 inches, turrets 2 inches, conning tower 4 inches
DIMENSIONS: length 556 feet (overall), beam 62 feet, draught $16\frac{1}{2}$ feet

(3) LEANDER CLASS
Orion: Captain G. R. B. Back
7,215 tons, $32\frac{1}{2}$ knots, eight 6-inch
Completed at Devonport 1932; scrapped 1949

Ajax: Captain E. D. B. McCarthy
6,985 tons, $32\frac{1}{2}$ knots, eight 6-inch
Completed at Barrow 1934: *Graf Spee* battle 1939; scrapped 1949

Perth, RAN (ex-*Amphion*): Captain Sir P. W. Bowyer-Smith, Bart. 7,165 tons, $32\frac{1}{2}$ knots, eight 6-inch

Completed at Portsmouth 1934; transferred to RAN 1940; sunk in Java Sea battle 1942

Displacement and main armament as above

ADDITIONAL ARMAMENT: eight 4-inch AA, eight 2 pdr (not in *Perth*), twelve 20mm, eight 21-inch torpedo tubes, one float-plane and catapult

PROPULSION: 4-shaft geared turbines SHP 72,000 = $32\frac{1}{2}$ knots

COMPLEMENT: 550

PROTECTION: main belt 4 inches, deck 2 inches, turrets and conning tower 1 inch

DIMENSIONS: length 555 feet (overall), beam 56 feet, draught 16 feet

RADAR: *Orion* early type ASV; *Ajax* type 279; *Perth* nil

(4) DIDO CLASS

Dido: Captain H. W. V. McCall
5,450 tons, 33 knots, ten 5.25-inch
Completed at Cammell Laird 1938; scrapped 1958

Naiad: Captain M. H. A. Kelsey, DSC
5,450 tons, 33 knots, ten 5.25-inch
Completed at Hawthorn Leslie 1939; lost March 11th, 1942

Phoebe: Captain G. Grantham
5,450 tons, 33 knots, ten 5.25-inch, but Q turret later removed
Completed at Fairfield 1939; scrapped 1956

ADDITIONAL ARMAMENT: eight 2 pdr AA, eight 0.5-inch, six 21-inch torpedo tubes

PROPULSION: 4-shaft geared turbines SHP 62,000 = 33 knots

COMPLEMENT: 550

PROTECTION: main belt 3 inches, deck 2 inches, turrets 2 inches, conning tower 1 inch

DIMENSIONS: length 512 feet (overall), beam 50 feet, draught 14 feet

(5) CAPETOWN CLASS

Calcutta: Captain D. M. Lees, DSO
4,290 tons, 29 knots, eight 4-inch, four 2 pdr, eight 0.5-inch
Completed at Armstrong Vickers 1918; lost at Crete

Carlisle: Captain T. C. Hampton
4,290 tons, 29 knots, eight 4-inch, four 2-pdr, eight 0.5-inch
Completed at Fairfield 1918; scrapped 1949

PROPULSION: 2-shaft geared turbines SHP 40,000 = 29 knots

COMPLEMENT: 400

PROTECTION: main belt 3 inches, deck 1 inch, conning tower 3 inches
DIMENSIONS: length 452 feet (overall), beam $43\frac{1}{2}$ feet, draught $14\frac{1}{4}$ feet

(6) CERES CLASS
Coventry: Captain W. P. Carne
4,190 tons, 29 knots, ten 4-inch, sixteen 2 pdr
Completed at Swan Hunter 1917; lost September 14th, 1942
Note: Apart from armament the particulars are as for the Capetown class, but without the trawler bows

(E) CRUISER MINELAYER: Abdiel class
Abdiel: Captain Hon. E. Pleydell-Bouverie, MVO
Completed at White 1940; lost September 9th, 1943
2,650 tons, 40 knots, six 4.7-inch, four 2 pdr, eight 0.5-inch, 160 mines
PROPULSION: 2-shaft geared turbines, SHP 72,000 = 40 knots
COMPLEMENT: 250
PROTECTION: nil
DIMENSIONS: length 418 feet (overall), beam 40 feet, draught $11\frac{1}{4}$ feet

(F) DESTROYERS: 'V', 'W', 'Scott', 'D', 'G', 'H', 'I', 'Tribal', 'J', 'K', and 'N' classes
(1) 'V' AND 'W' CLASSES
Vampire, RAN, 10th DF: Commander J. A. Walsh
1,100 tons, 34 knots, four 4-inch
Completed at White 1917; lost April 9th, 1942

Vendetta, RAN, 10th DF: Lieut-Cdr R. Rhoades
1,100 tons, 34 knots, four 4-inch
Completed at Fairfield 1917; scuttled off Sydney 1948

Voyager, RAN, 10th DF: Commander J. C. Morrow, DSO
1,100 tons, 34 knots, four 4-inch
Completed at Stephen 1918; lost September 25th, 1942

Waterhen, RAN, 10th DF: Lieut-Cdr J. H. Swain
1,100 tons, 34 knots, four 4-inch
Completed at Palmers 1918; lost June 30th, 1941
ADDITIONAL ARMAMENT: one 12 pdr and 2/4 20mm AA
TORPEDO TUBES: six 21-inch
PROPULSION: 2-shaft geared turbines SHP 27,000 = 34 knots,

COMPLEMENT: 134
PROTECTION: nil
DIMENSIONS: length 312 feet (overall), beam $29\frac{1}{2}$ feet, draught $8\frac{1}{2}$ feet

(2) 'SCOTT' CLASS
Stuart, RAN, 10th DF: Captain H. M. L. Waller, DSO, RAN, Captain D 10
1,530 tons, $36\frac{1}{2}$ knots, five 4.7-inch, one 3-inch HA
Completed at Hawthorn Leslie 1918; transferred to RAN 1932; Mediterranean 1941; returned to Australia for vast repairs 1941; scrapped at Sydney 1947
TORPEDO TUBES: six 21-inch
PROPULSION: 2-shaft geared turbines SHP 40,000 = $36\frac{1}{2}$ knots
COMPLEMENT: 183
PROTECTION: nil
DIMENSIONS: length $332\frac{1}{2}$ feet (overall), beam $31\frac{3}{4}$ feet, draught $9\frac{1}{4}$ feet

(3) 'D' CLASS
Decoy, 10th DF: Commander E. G. McGregor, DSO
1,375 tons, $35\frac{1}{2}$ knots, four 4-inch
Completed at Thornycroft 1932; RCN 1943; scrapped 1946

Defender, 10th DF: Lieut-Cdr G. L. Farnfield
1,375 tons, $35\frac{1}{2}$ knots, four 4-inch
Completed at Barrow 1932; lost July 11th, 1941
ADDITIONAL ARMAMENT: two 2 pdr AA, eight 0.5-inch AA
TORPEDO TUBES: eight 21-inch
PROPULSION: 2-shaft turbines SHP 36,000 = $35\frac{1}{2}$ knots
COMPLEMENT: 145
PROTECTION: nil
DIMENSIONS: length 329 feet (overall), beam 33 feet, draught $8\frac{1}{2}$ feet

(4) 'G' AND 'H' CLASSES
Greyhound, 14th DF: Commander W. R. Marshall-A'Deane, DSO, DSC
1,335 tons, 36 knots, four 4.7-inch, one 3-inch HA
Completed at Barrow 1935; lost at Crete May 22nd, 1941

Griffin, 14th DF: Lieutenant K. R. C. Letts
1,335 tons, 36 knots, four 4.7-inch, one 3-inch HA
Completed at Barrow 1935; transferred to RCN 1942

Hasty, 2nd DF: Lieut-Cdr L. R. K. Tyrwhitt
1,340 tons, 36 knots, four 4.7-inch
Completed at Denny 1936; lost June 15th, 1942

Hereward, 2nd DF: Lieutenant W. J. Munn
1,340, 36 knots, four 4.7-inch
Completed at Tyne 1936; lost at Crete May 29th, 1941

Havock, 2nd DF: Lieutenant G. R. G. Watkins
1,340 tons, 36 knots, four 4,7-inch
Completed at Denny 1936; lost April 6th, 1942

Hotspur, 2nd DF: Lieut-Cdr C. P. F. Brown, DSC
1,340 tons, 36 knots, four 4.7-inch
Completed at Scotts 1936; transferred to Dominica 1948

Hero, 2nd DF: Commander H. W. Biggs, DSO
1,340 tons, 36 knots, four 4.7-inch
Completed on the Tyne 1936; transferred to RCN 1943
TORPEDO TUBES: eight 21-inch
ANTI-AIRCRAFT armament was augmented by eight 0.5-inch
PROPULSION: 2-shaft geared turbines SHP 34,000 = 36 knots
COMPLEMENT: 145
PROTECTION: nil
DIMENSIONS: length 323 feet (overall), beam $32\frac{1}{4}$ feet, draught $8\frac{1}{2}$ feet

(5) 'I' CLASS
Ilex, 2nd DF: Captain H. St. L. Nicholson, DSO; Captain D 2
1,370 tons, 36 knots, four 4.7-inch
Completed at Clydebank 1937; scrapped 1948

Isis, 2nd DF: Commander C. S. B. Swinley, DSO
1,370 tons, 36 knots, four 4.7-inch
Completed at Yarrow 1936; lost July 20th, 1944

Imperial, 2nd DF: Lieut-Cdr C. A. De W. Kitcat
1,370 tons, 36 knots, four 4.7-inch
Completed at Hawthorn Leslie 1936; lost May 29th, 1941
TORPEDO TUBES: ten 21-inch
Remaining details as for 'G' and 'H' classes (except for displacement
of 1,370 tons)

(6) 'TRIBAL' CLASS
Nubian, 14th DF: Commander R. W. Ravenhill

1,870 tons, 36½ knots, eight 4.7-inch
Completed at Thornycroft 1937; stern blown off at Crete May 26th, 1941; scrapped 1949

TORPEDO TUBES: four 21-inch

ANTI-AIRCRAFT armament augmented by four 2 pdr and eight 0.5-inch AA

PROPULSION: 2-shaft geared turbines SHP 44,000 = 36 knots

COMPLEMENT: 190

PROTECTION: nil

DIMENSIONS: length 377½ feet (overall), beam 36½ feet, draught 9 feet

Note: The large Tribal class, with increased gun armament and reduced torpedo armament, was Britain's response to the large destroyers building abroad. Stress was laid on anti-submarine capability. The twin 4.7-inch mounting was introduced.

(7) 'J' AND 'K' CLASSES

Jervis, 14th DF: Captain P. J. Mack, DSO; Captain D 14
1,760 tons, 36 knots, six 4.7-inch, one 4-inch HA
Completed at Hawthorn Leslie 1938; scrapped 1949

Janus, 14th DF: Commander J. A. W. Tothill, DSC
1,760 tons, 36 knots, six 4.7-inch, one 4-inch HA
Completed at Wallsend 1938; lost 1944

Jaguar, 14th DF: Lieut-Cdr J. F. W. Hine
1,760 tons, 36 knots, six 4.7-inch, one 4-inch HA
Completed at Denny 1938; lost March 26th, 1942

Juno, 14th DF: Commander St. J. R. J. Tyrwhitt
1,760 tons, 36 knots, six 4.7-inch, one 4-inch HA
Completed at Fairfield 1938; lost May 21st, 1941

Kandahar, 14th DF: Commander W. G. A. Robson, DSO
1,760 tons, 36 knots, six 4.7-inch, one 4-inch HA
Completed at Denny 1939; lost December 20th 1941

Kimberley, 14th DF: Lieut-Cdr J. S. M. Richardson, DSO
1,760 tons, 36 knots, six 4.7-inch, one 4-inch HA
Completed at Thornycroft 1939; scrapped 1949

Kingston, 14th DF: Lieut-Cdr P. Somerville, DSO, DSC
1,760 tons, 36 knots, six 4.7-inch, one 4-inch HA
Completed at White 1939; scrapped 1942

Kelly, 5th DF: Captain Lord Louis Mountbatten, GCVO, DSO; Captain D 5
1,760 tons, 36 knots, six 4.7-inch, one 4-inch HA
Completed at Hawthorn Leslie 1938; lost May 23rd ,1941

Jackal, 5th DF: Lieut-Cdr R. M. P. Jonas
1,760 tons, 36 knots, six 4.7-inch, one 4-inch HA
Completed at Clydebank 1938; lost May 12th, 1942

Kelvin, 5th DF: Commander J. H. Alison, DSO
1,760 tons, 36 knots, six 4.7-inch, one 4-inch HA
Completed at Fairfield 1939; scrapped 1949

Kashmir, 5th DF: Commander H. A. King
1,760 tons, 36 knots, six 4.7-inch, one 4-inch HA
Completed at Thornycroft 1939; lost at Crete May 23rd, 1941

Kipling, 5th DF: Commander A. St Clair-Ford
1,760 tons, 36 knots, six 4.7-inch, one 4-inch HA
Completed Yarrow 1939; lost May 11th, 1942
TORPEDO TUBES: ten 21-inch
ANTI-AIRCRAFT armament augmented by four 2 pdr and eight 0.5-inch AA
PROPULSION: 2-shaft geared turbines; SHP 40,000=36 knots
COMPLEMENT: 183 (218 in *Jervis* and *Kelly*)
PROTECTION: nil
DIMENSIONS: length 356½ feet (overall), beam 36 feet, draught 9 feet
Note: Owing to expense, one of the twin gun mountings of the Tribal class was suppressed in the 'J' and 'K' classes, in favour of increased AA and torpedo armament. There was also a reduction to two boilers, resulting in a single funnel profile for the 'J' and 'K' classes. Tripod foremast and no mainmast.

(8) 'N' CLASS
Napier, RAN, 7th DF: Captain S. H. T. Arliss; Captain D 7
1,760 tons, 36 knots, six 4.7-inch
Completed at Fairfield 1940; RAN (1940-45), scrapped 1956

Nizam, RAN, 7th DF: Lieut-Cdr M. J. Clark, RAN
1,760 tons, 36 knots, six 4.7-inch
Completed at Clydebank 1940; RAN (1941-45), scrapped 1955
Details as for 'J' and 'K' classes, except for the fitting of two 20mm AA in the bridge wings.

(G) MINELAYING SUBMARINE—Porpoise class
Rorqual: Commander R. H. Dewhurst, DSO
1,500/2,000 tons, 15/9 knots, one 4-inch, six 21-inch TT, 50 mines
Completed at Barrow 1936; scrapped 1946
Complement: 59

(H) SLOOPS

(1) GRIMSBY CLASS
Grimsby: Commander K. J. D'arcy
990 tons, $16\frac{1}{2}$ knots, two 4.7-inch, one 3-inch AA
Completed at Devonport 1933; May 25th 1941
Complement: 100

(2) EGRET CLASS
Auckland: Commander J. G. Hewitt, DSO
1,200 tons, $19\frac{1}{4}$ knots, eight 4-inch, four 0.5-inch AA
Completed at Denny 1938; lost June 24th, 1941
Complement: 188

(3) BLACK SWAN CLASS
Flamingo: Commander J. H. Huntley
1,250 tons, $19\frac{1}{4}$ knots, six 4-inch, four 2 pdr AA, four 0.5-inch
Completed at Yarrow 1939; to West Germany 1958

(I) CORVETTE—Flower class
Salvia: Lieut-Cdr J. I. Miller, DSO, DSC, RD, RNR
926 tons, 16 knots, one 4-inch, four 0.5-inch AA
Completed at Simons 1940; lost December 24th, 1941

(J) SPECIAL SERVICE SHIPS
Glenroy: Captain Sir James Paget, Bart (ret)

Glengyle: Captain C. H. Petrie (ret)

(K) MINESWEEPERS
Widnes: Lieut-Cdr R. B. Chandler, RN. Sunk at Crete

Derby: Lieutenant F. C. V. Brightman, RN

(L) PATROL CRAFT
KOS 21: Lieut-Cdr I. H. Wilson, SAN
KOS 22: Lieutenant H. D. Foxon, RNR. Sunk at Crete
KOS 23: Lieut-Cdr J. J. Reid, RNVR. Sunk at Crete
SYVERN: Lieut-Cdr R. E. Clarke, RNR. Sunk at Crete
MOONSTONE: Lieut-Cdr P. G. Britten, RNR
LANNER: Skipper W. Stewart, RNR

(M) MOTOR LAUNCHES
ML 1011: Lieutenant A. H. Blake, RNR. Sunk at Crete
ML 1030: Lieutenant W. M. O. Cooksey, RNVR. Sunk at Crete
ML 1032: Lieutenant E. N. Rose, RNVR

(N) MOTOR TORPEDO BOATS
MTB 67: sunk at Crete
MTB 213: Lieutenant G. L. Cotton, RNVR. Sunk at Crete
MTB 314: sunk at Crete
MTB 216: Lieutenant C. L. Coles, RNVR. Sunk at Crete
MTB 217: sunk at Crete

Greek Navy: The Greeks lost many ships both warships and cargo ships, but these were mainly sunk by the Germans in Greek ports.

Italian Navy: Two torpedo boats of the Italian Navy (mentioned in the narrative) attempted to escort German troop convoys to Crete. Details are as follows:

TORPEDO BOATS
SPICA CLASS
Lupo: Commander Francesco Mimbelli
Completed at Fiume 1938; sunk December 2nd, 1942

Sagittario: Lieutenant Giuseppe Cigala Fulgosi
Completed at Fiume 1936; discarded 1964
DISPLACEMENT: 1,000 tons
ARMAMENT: three 4-inch, ten 20mm, four 17.7-inch torpedo tubes
PROPULSION: 2-shaft geared turbines, SHP 19,000＝30 knots
COMPLEMENT: 120
DIMENSIONS: length 80m, beam 8m, draught $2\frac{1}{2}$m

Gun Defences in Crete

Maleme Airfield
A two-gun 4-inch battery, a two-gun 3-inch battery, and 10 Bofors (AA)
Suda Area
Four 6-inch, two 4-inch, eight 3.7-inch (AA), ten 3-inch (AA), one 12 pdr, eight 0.5-inch (AA), and 16 Bofors (AA)
Armyro Beach (near Georgioupolis)
A two-gun 4-inch battery
Heraklion
A two-gun 4-inch battery and two 2 pdr at the harbour. Four 3-inch (AA) and ten Bofors (AA) at the airfield

Chronology of Events

Wednesday May 14th, 1941
am: Heavy German air attacks on Heraklion and Maleme airfields.
pm: Force A under Pridham-Wippell sails from Alexandria to cover waters west of Crete.
       Wellingtons raid Menidi and Hassani airfields in Greece.
Friday May 16th
am: Force B (*Gloucester* and *Fiji*) take 2nd Bn. Leicester Regt to Crete.
       Heavy air attacks on Maleme and Heraklion airfields, and at Suda Bay and Canea.
pm: Force C and Force D (cruisers and destroyers) operating in readiness to sweep Aegean.

Saturday May 17th

am: Sud**a** Bay bombed by Ju87s.

      Heavy air raids on Maleme and Heraklion airfields, and on Suda, continue.

      RAF attack with night fighters on airfields at Hassani, Argos, and Malaoli.

pm: Cruisers and destroyers recalled to Alexandria for refuelling and replenishment.

Sunday May 18th

am: Heavy air raids on Suda Bay, and Maleme and Heraklion airfields.

pm: *Glengyle* lands 700 Argyll and Sutherland Highlanders at Tymbaki.

      Wellingtons bomb Hassani and Eleusis airfields in Greece.

Monday May 19th

    Bombing and low flying machine-gun attacks on Maleme and Heraklion airfields all day.

    Dive bombing on Suda Bay at 08.00hrs and 19.15hrs.

    Rawlings with Force A1 relieves Force A south-west of Crete.

    Three 'I' tanks landed at Tymbaki.

Tuesday May 20th

AIRBORNE ASSAULT BEGINS

am: Heavy bombing in Maleme and Suda areas precedes glider and parachute landings.

      Forces A1, B, and D to westward of Crete; Force C to southward of Kaso Strait.

pm: Parachute landings at Heraklion and Retimo.

Wednesday May 21st

am: Situation at Maleme and Canea still in hand.

      Cruisers and destroyers patrolling north and north-west of Crete.

      Three destroyers bombard Scarpanto airfield before dawn.

      Savage air bombardment in Maleme-Canea area. German troop carriers landed regardless of losses. Enemy concentrate near Canea, and immediately west of Maleme airfield.

pm: Maleme airfield captured by enemy.

Successful counter-attacks at Retimo and Heraklion.

Forces A1, B, and D to westward of Crete. Force C to south-ward of Kaso.

Juno sunk by air attack.

Glennie's force destroys trooping caiques north of Canea.

Thursday May 22nd

am: New Zealand counter-attack, before dawn, reaches Maleme airfield. Forced to withdraw.

pm: Situation deteriorates; withdrawal to new line. Large enemy airborne reinforcements. Heraklion situation well in hand; many aircraft destroyed.

King's force encounters convoy south of Milos; heavily attacked by aircraft; *Naiad* and *Carlisle* damaged; joined by Rawlings's battle squadron in Kithera Channel. *Greyhound*, *Gloucester*, *Fiji* sunk. *Warspite* and *Valiant* hit by bombs.

Friday May 23rd

am: *Kelly* and *Kashmir* sink caiques north of Crete, and bombard Maleme.

King of Greece leaves Crete in *Decoy*.

Wellingtons drop medical stores and supplies at Heraklion and Retimo.

At 04.08hrs Cunningham orders all naval forces to withdraw to Alexandria for replenishment, under the mistaken impression (caused by corrupt signal) that forces are out of close-range AA ammunition.

Blenheims bomb Maleme at dawn.

Naval forces return to Alexandria.

Kashmir and *Kelly* sunk by 24 dive bombers.

The five MTBs in Suda Bay sunk by air attack.

New line formed east of Maleme in Maleme-Canea sector suffers very heavy air attacks. Steady flow of enemy reinforcements in troop carriers.

pm: At Heraklion ultimatum demanding surrender is rejected by British and Greek Commanders.

Saturday May 24th

Before dawn, *Jaguar* and *Defender* disembark ammunition in Suda Bay.

At dawn, Wellingtons bomb enemy aircraft at Maleme: three Wellingtons lost. Five Hurricanes machine-gun enemy positions near Heraklion.

Canea British Army Headquarters transfer to Naval Headquarters Suda, owing to very heavy bombing.

Fighting continues in Maleme-Canea area.

At Heraklion, Greeks short of ammunition.

Cunningham informs Chiefs-of-Staff that scale of air attack too great for Navy to operate in the Aegean or vicinity of Crete during daylight.

Sunday May 25th

Before dawn, cruisers and destroyers sweep north coast of Crete.

At dawn, Wellingtons drop medical stores at Retimo.

All day, continuous air attacks west of Canea. Enemy captures Galatas: British and New Zealand troops recapture it.

Troop carriers pour in enemy reinforcements.

Blenheims, Hurricanes, and Marylands bomb and machine-gun German aircraft on Maleme airfield, destroying about 24. One Maryland, three Blenheims, and three Hurricanes missing.

Monday May 26th

am: Before dawn, light cruisers and destroyers repeat sweep.

At dawn, *Formidable*'s air squadrons attack Scarpanto airfield. Line formed in Canea-Maleme sector broken after repeated attacks, forcing Imperial troops to fall back on Canea. At Heraklion, two 'I' tanks and Argyll and Sutherland Highlanders break through from south; large numbers of enemy successfully held.

pm: Pridham-Wippell's Force attacked by 20 aircraft from African coast; *Formidable* and *Nubian* severely damaged.

Tuesday May 27th

Before dawn, *Abdiel* and two destroyers land 750 special service troops and stores at Suda. *Glenroy* with reinforcements recalled to Alexandria.

Pridham-Wippell's Force bombed; *Barham* hit. Force recalled to Alexandria.

Suda defence line collapses suddenly, and withdrawal begins.

At 08.24hrs, Wavell informs PM that Crete is no longer tenable.

Chiefs of Staff order evacuation.

AOC Middle East promises all possible fighter protection for Cunningham's ships.

Troops from Suda line, retreat in some disorder towards Sphakia. Major-General Weston assumes command of rearguard.

Heraklion sector still holding out, but major attack by Germans expected.

Wednesday May 28th

At 06.00hrs, Rawlings with Force B (3 cruisers, 6 destroyers) leaves Alexandria for Heraklion.

At 08.00hrs Captain Arliss with Force C (4 destroyers) sails for Sphakia.

Joint Naval and Military Headquarters in cave at Sphakia. Retreat to Sphakia continues.

Enemy reinforcements dropped in the Heraklion area.

Four Wellingtons bomb 100 aircraft on ground at Maleme.

Four Wellingtons bomb Scarpanto airfield.

At 20.00hrs *Ajax* bombed; detached to Alexandria.

Thursday May 29th

am: Before dawn, Force C embarks 700 troops at Sphakia, and Force B embarks 4,000 troops at Heraklion; *Imperial* sunk on leaving.

At 06.00hrs and thereafter till 15.00hrs, Force B heavily attacked by aircraft. *Hereward* lost; *Orion* and *Dido* hit; considerable casualties.

Rearguard under Weston carrying out orderly retreat.

pm: Sphakia heavily bombed and machine-gunned.

Forces B and C arrive Alexandria.

Rear-Admiral King with Force D (2 cruisers, *Glengyle*, 2 AA cruisers, 3 destroyers) on passage to Sphakia from Alexandria. After interviews with officers returned from Crete, Cunningham decides to continue evacuation 30/31.

RAF aircraft sent to order troops at Retimo to Plaka fails to return; Cunningham decides to send no ships to Plaka.

Friday May 30th

am: Before dawn, Force D embarks 6,000 men at Sphakia.

At dawn, Wellingtons bomb Scarpanto, Rhodes, and Maleme.

From dawn onwards, the rearguard carry out successful delaying action aided by two light tanks and three bren gun carriers, only a few miles north of Sphakia.

pm: Force D arrives Alexandria. RAF provided fighters most of day, but *Perth* hit by bomb on passage.

Captain Arliss with Force C (two destroyers) on passage to Sphakia.

Creforce requests last lift from Sphakia, before dawn June 1st, for 3,000 men.

Saturday May 31st

am: Before dawn, Force C embarks 1,500 men at Sphakia. Fighter protection for Force C accounts for three Ju88s, one Cant.

Before dawn, Freyberg and Morse return to Egypt in Sunderland. Weston in command in Crete. His estimate of numbers remaining near Sphakia:

Fighting troops	..	4,000
Mixed formations	..	3,500
Scattered	..	1,500
Grand total	..	9,000

At 06.00hrs, King in *Phoebe* with *Abdiel* and three destroyers on passage to Sphakia for final lift.

pm: Force C arrives Alexandria. *Napier* damaged by near miss on passage.

Admiralty informed that evacuation will cease after dawn June 1st. Weston also informed, by Wavell, in a personal message which authorises capitulation of troops remaining in Crete on June 1st.

Sunday June 1st

Before dawn, King's Force D embarks nearly 4,000 troops at Sphakia, and receives RAF fighter protection on passage to Alexandria.

Weston orders senior British officer remaining in Crete to capitulate, and returns to Egypt in Sunderland, as ordered.

At 09.20hrs *Calcutta* dive-bombed and sunk while on passage to meet King's Force D.

At 17.00hrs, Force D arrives at Alexandria after uneventful passage. Admiralty informed evacuation terminated.

Note: Ships of the Mediterranean Fleet remaining fit for service were as follows: 2 battleships, 1 cruiser, 1 AA cruiser, 1 minelayer and 9 destroyers.

APPENDIX E

Results of Bomb Attacks on H.M. Ships

DB = Dive bomb; HL = High level; LL = Low level

Date	Attacks	Aircraft shot down or damaged	Ship	Resulting Damage	Out of Action
May 21	26 HL	7	Juno	Sunk	—
			Ajax	Near miss: shaft distortion	3 months
				Bow bent through ramming caique	
May 22	67 DB	11	Greyhound	Sunk	—
			Gloucester	Sunk	—
			Fiji	Sunk	—
			Naiad	4 near misses: structural	3 weeks
			Carlisle	2 hits: funnel and No 2 gun	1 month
			Perth	Near miss: 6-inch fire control	4½ months
			Warspite	1,000lb bomb: starboard side	7 months
			Valiant	2 hits aft: not serious	nil
			Kingston	Near miss: machinery and hull	1 week

Date	Attacks	Aircraft shot down or damaged	Ship	Resulting Damage	Out of Action
May 23	32 DB	9	Havock	Near miss: boiler room	3 weeks
			Ilex	Near miss: propeller	4 days
			Kelly	Sunk	—
			Kashmir	Sunk	—
May 24	3	nil		nil	
May 25	6	nil		nil	
May 26	40 DB	4	Formidable	Hit starboard side forward and aft: fo'c'sle and turrets	6 months
			Nubian	Hit aft: stern blown off	17 months
May 27	40 DB	6	Barham	Hit on Y turret: near miss floods two bulges	2 months
May 28	13	nil	Ajax	Hit augmenting damage of 21 May	3 months
May 29	40 DB	1	Imperial	Steering trouble: sunk by Hotspur	—
			Hereward	Sunk	—
			Orion	2 hits: A turret and bridge	8½ months
			Dido	Hit on B turret	5 months
			Decoy	Near miss: reduction in speed	—
May 30	4 HL & DB	1	Perth	Hit	4½ months
			Kelvin	Near miss	6½ months

Date	Attacks	Aircraft shot down or damaged	Ship	Resulting Damage	Out of Action
May 31	4 DB	5	Napier	Near miss: machinery damage	6 weeks
			Nizam	Near miss: machinery damage	1 week
June 1	1 DB	nil	Calcutta	Sunk	—

Note: The figure of enemy aircraft shot down does not include those intercepted by RAF fighters before their attacks could develop.

APPENDIX F

Number of Troops Disembarked at Alexandria

Date	HM Ships	From	Number
Prior to May 27	—	—	112
May 27	Abdiel, Hero, Nizam	Suda	930
May 29	Force B (Rawlings): Orion Dido, Kimberley, Decoy, Jackal, Hotspur	Heraklion	3,486
	Force C (Arliss): Napier, Nizam, Kelvin, Kandahar	Sphakia	680

Date	HM Ships	From	Number
May 30	Force D (King): *Phoebe, Glengyle, Perth, Jervis, Janus, Hasty*	Spharkia	6,029
May 31	Force C (Arliss): *Napier, Nizam*	Sphakia	1,510
June 1	Force D (King): *Phoebe, Abdiel, Jackal, Hotspur, Kimberley*	Sphakia	3,710
	By Sunderland	Sphakia	54
			16,511

Figures are only approximate. Those killed on passage are not included, and it is believed that the total evacuated from Crete is about 17,000.

APPENDIX G

Lessons from Battle of Crete

Note: At this distance in time, some of the lessons pronounced by Commander-in-Chief Middle East in June 1941 may sound platitudinous, but it is important to remember that this was one of the earliest airborne assaults, and it had been only narrowly successful.

(a) Aerodromes being enemy main objectives must be organised for all-round defence (including Pill Boxes), specially as parachutists may drop behind defences. Defences, including artillery, must be in depth. Artillery in sites with cover proved more useful than those in open with all-round field of fire.

(b) All ranks of all arms must be armed with rifles and bayonets and high proportion of Tommy guns to protect themselves and, in the case of Artillery, their guns.

(c) By day it should be easy to deal with parachutists, but it must be remembered that parachutists may land at night and secure an aerodrome. Main problem is to deal with enemy airborne troops, and as it is impossible to be strong everywhere, there must be strong mobile reserves, centrally placed, preferably with tanks.

(d) Defence must be offensive. Immediate action by mobile reserves essential to prevent enemy settling down, and in order to secure quick action, good system of intercommunication is vital. Delay may allow enemy air to prevent movement.

(e) During bombing phase, AA and LMGs should remain silent unless required to protect own aircraft on the ground.

(f) AA lay-out should include dummy AA guns and alternative positions. Positions of AA guns should be continually changed.

(g) Arrangements must be made quickly to render aerodromes liable to attack temporarily unfit for landing.

(h) Equally important to quick action of mobile reserves is position of fighter aircraft support, the existence of which might prevent any airborne landing from succeeding, or at least reduce enemy effort.

Foregoing are interim lessons, which may be modified as result of views of special inter-services Committee examining operations.
(Extract from signal made by Commander-in-Chief Middle East 6 June 1941)

Losses at Crete

(A) Royal Navy
(1) Officers and men: 1,828 killed, 183 wounded
(2) Ships:

Sunk
3 cruisers (*Gloucester, Fiji, Calcutta*)
6 destroyers (*Juno, Greyhound, Kelly, Kashmir, Imperial, Hereward*)
Damaged
4 capital ships (*Warspite, Barham, Valiant, Formidable*)
6 cruisers (*Ajax, Naiad, Perth, Orion, Dido, Carlisle*)
7 destroyers (*Kelvin, Nubian, Napier, Ilex, Havock, Kingston, Nizam*)

(B) Allied Troops
Original total 32,000

Evacuated from Crete to Alexandria	..			..	17,000
Later escapes	..	..	..	..	1,000
Killed	..	..	..	..	1,800
Taken prisoner	..	..	..	..	12,000
		Approximate Total		..	31,800

(C) Royal Air Force
23 bombers with crews lost
23 fighters with crews lost

(D) Luftwaffe
Killed and wounded:
    4,000 (estimate provided by Germans)
    17,000 (estimate given by General Freyberg)
Note: See Chapter 12 for comment on these figures
Total aircraft losses: 220 (including fighters, bombers, and reconnaissance and transport planes)

The Influence of Air Power on Sea Power

(A) The Importance of the Carrier

After the battle for Crete Cunningham wrote 'The struggle in no way proved that the air is master over the sea. The proper way to fight the air is in the air.'* He warned that there should be no hasty conclusion that ships are impotent in the face of air attack. His unceasing appeal for more 'air' has already been described in Chapter 12, together with the limitations imposed by an all-round shortage of aircraft and difficulties of transporting them from home. The presence of a few RAF fighters, when they were able to attend Cunningham's ships in the last few days of the evacuation from Sphakia, made a considerable difference, and permitted the ships in some cases to complete their passage unhindered. Alternatively, Cunningham would have been content with two or three modern aircraft carriers armed with a full complement of serviceable fighters and bombers. By virtue of their design for fleet use, the carrier-based aircraft was unlikely to match the performance of shore-based aircraft, but the great advantage was that they were flown by naval men who were familiar with ships and the sea, and moreover were under the Commander-in-Chief's complete control. In the event, he was more often without either carrier-based or shore-based aircraft. Pre-war policy for defence in certain areas had worked on the assumption that the fleet and shipping would not be far from certain shore bases from which aircraft could provide protection. In the Royal Navy itself there had been, between the wars, a certain apathy towards 'air'. As late as 1940 there were still many naval officers who regarded the battleship as the primary unit of strength. In their eyes all other units existed for roles complementary to the paramountcy of the big ship.

In spite of setbacks suffered by the Fleet Air Arm of the Royal Navy during the years 1918 to 1937, whilst removed from effectual control by the Admiralty, that Arm made a remarkable recovery

* *A Sailor's Odyssey*, p 391

om 1937 onwards, growing from a small force into a weapon whose full potential of patrol, reconnaissance, offence, and defence in a fleet action was first realised at Matapan. Taranto, a few months earlier, had demonstrated also the great offensive potential of this long-range weapon launched from a mobile base providing the indispensable strategical and tactical factors of flexibility and surprise.

The lessons were not lost on the Japanese, who were to have their own Taranto at Pearl Harbour before 1941 was ended. Nor were they lost on the Italians, but it was already too late for them to do anything effectual. Britain was pitifully weak in the number of modern carriers she possessed, and in aircraft and airmen to operate them; the carrier was always singled out for destruction and became the centre and prime target of enemy attacks. Britain began the war with a collection of vulnerable carriers, the old *Argus*, *Eagle*, *Hermes*, *Courageous*, *Glorious*, *Furious*, and the new *Ark Royal*. Of these only the *Argus* and *Furious* survived the war.

Thanks to the foresight of a former First Sea Lord, Lord Chatfield, six carriers with armoured flight deck were on order at the outbreak of war. *Illustrious* became operational by August 1940, *Formidable* November 1940, *Victorious* May 1941, *Indomitable* December 1941, *Indefatigable* July 1944, and *Implacable* October 1944. Had we received them a year or two earlier, those tragic losses at Crete in May 1941 would probably not have happened.

A succession of escort carriers (as well as new aircraft) continued to flow in later years from USA for the Royal Navy, with such aggressive names as *Attacker*, *Biter*, *Chaser*, *Dasher*, *Fencer*, *Hunter*, *Pursuer*, *Striker*, followed by the 'Ruler' class of carriers. These were to play a great role of flexible and swift support exactly where required most. Without them our seaborne landings in the various spheres in the Mediterranean Sea in 1943 must have failed, especially those distant from shore bases. The Italian Air Force had the ear of Mussolini who supported their wish for independence from the Army and the Navy (as existed in Germany), and were rightly proud of their competence in high level bombing.

This independence led to a lack of understanding of naval requirements by the air force, and a failure to develop the aerial torpedo to any great extent, which our own Fleet Air Arm made such a formidable and effectual weapon, threatening even the heaviest and best protected battleships. Meanwhile the Germans continued to develop their deadly dive bombing technique.

Italian aircraft nevertheless compared favourably with German or British counterparts in 1941, as can be seen in the tables in the next section. It must be remembered however that the total of Italian and German air strength was overwhelmingly greater than that which the British could muster in the Mediterranean at the time.

(B) Relative Performance of Aircraft
(1) *General*
The figures given in (2) Fighters and (3) Bombers provide only a general guide, and must obviously vary with such factors as climate, wind, loading, altitude, extra tanks (LRT), and accuracy of navigation. This applies especially to what I have termed the Endurance Range, ie the distance that can be flown in still air until the tanks are empty. Endurance Range must not be confused with radius of action.

In view of the fact that distances over the sea are quoted in sea miles, all the endurance ranges are given in sea miles. (One sea mile equals 2,000 yards equal $1\frac{1}{7}$ statute miles. Hence 7 sea miles= 8 statute miles.)

For a similar reason all speeds are quoted in knots.

$$\left(7 \text{ knots} = \frac{8 \text{ statute miles}}{\text{hour}}\right)$$

(2) *Performance of Fighters* (see page 131)
(3) *Performance of Bombers* (see pages 132–133)

(C) The Luftwaffe in the Mediterranean
The Luftwaffe first arrived in the Mediterranean in January 1941 with the establishment of Fliegerkorps X in Sicily, with the object of attacking Malta and shipping passing through the narrows between Sicily and Tunis. Units of this body were detached to Libya to support Rommel, but not to come under his orders. Fliegerkorps X also played a part in the capture of Crete. But the operation was mainly carried out by Fliegerkorps VIII and Fliegerkorps XI, of which the former provided the reconnaissance, fighter, and bomber support, while the latter comprised all the airborne troops, gliders, parachutes, transport planes, and craft: in all about 22,000 men.

As soon as Crete was captured the crippled remains of the two Fliegerkorps VIII and XI were withdrawn, and Fliegerkorps X took up station to cover the Aegean and North Africa, with its headquarters in Greece. Aircraft in use were the single-engined dive bombers Ju87, the long-range bombers Ju88 and He111; and the fighters Me109 and Me110. Because of the scattered nature of airfields, about 80 Ju52 transport planes were maintained. Total strength was of the order of 400, of which only about a half were serviceable at any time.

(D) The Royal Air Force in the Mediterranean

By comparison the RAF total of serviceable planes for the Eastern Mediterranean was less than half of the German number, but new arrivals were continuing though spasmodically: 46 Hurricanes in May 1941, and 114 Hurricanes in June, brought by aircraft carrier from UK to within flying distance of Malta. The main route for delivery was however by sea to Takoradi and Lagos, a slow business owing to time expended in crating, uncrating, and erecting. Wellingtons and Beaufighters were able to fly direct or by Gibraltar and Malta. All aircraft flying in the desert had moreover first to be fitted with filters to the carburettor intakes. In performance it was found that the Hurricane could deal with all Italian types and could out-manoeuvre the Me110. Its chief defect was that it lacked range.

Our defeat at Crete certainly emphasised the crucial need for 'air' and probably did much to help the gradual build-up that took place in the following year.

APPENDIX J

Destroyer Endurance Range

The following table gives details of speed, fuel consumption, and range of the destroyer classes involved off Crete. Of the ten G, H, I class destroyers which took part, only three attained the designed 36 knots on trials, whereas all the 'J's and 'K's exceeded 36 knots. *Ilex* was a special case, with a different boiler arrangement; she was rather slower and appreciably heavier on fuel than her sisters. The 'Full Authorised' speed was that expected at deep load, six months out of dock.

(2) Relative Performance of Aircraft (Fighters)

Type	Armament	Crew	Fuel (gallons)	Economical Speed (Knots)	Maximum Speed (Knots)	Endurance Range (sea miles)	Nationality
Beaufighter Twin Engine Monoplane	6 × .303 4 × 20mm	2	550	200 at 15,000 ft	287 at 11,750 ft	1,335	British—RAF
Hurricane I Single Engine Monoplane	8 × .303	1	97	160 at 15,000 ft	280 at 17,750 ft	528	British—RAF
Fulmar Single Engine Monoplane	8 × .303	2	155	150 at 10,000 ft	200 at 10,000 ft	722	British—RN (Fleet Air Arm)
Me 109 E Single Engine Monoplane	2 × 7.9mm 3 × 20mm	1	88	176 at 16,500 ft	312 at 18,000 ft	575	German
Me 110 Twin Engine Monoplane	6 × 7.9mm 2 × 20mm	2	280	176 at 18,000 ft	317 at 20,000 ft	820	German
C.R. 42 Single Engine Biplane	2 × 12.7mm	1	535	132 at 13,100 ft	238 at 13,100 ft	470	Italian

(3) Relative Performance of Aircraft (Bombers)

Type	Armament	Crew	Bomb-load (lbs)	Economical Speed (Knots)	Maximum Speed (Knots)	Endurance Range (sea miles)	Nationality
Blenheim I Twin Engine Monoplane	2×.303	3	1,000	145 at 15,000 ft	234 at 15,000 ft	810	British—RAF
Wellington I Twin Engine Monoplane	6×.303	6	1,000 or 4,500	145 at 10,000 ft	200 at 4,700 ft	2,250 or 1,160	British—RAF
Albacore Single Engine Biplane	2×.303	3 or 2*	1,500 or Torpedo	100 at 6,000 ft	144 at 4,800 ft	460 or 850*	British— Fleet Air Arm *Use of Long-range Tank.
Swordfish Single Engine Biplane	2×.303	2	1,500 or Torpedo	90 at 5,000 ft	120 at 5,000 ft	465	British— Fleet Air Arm (nicknamed STRINGBAG)
Ju 87 (Stuka) Single Engine Monoplane	3×7.9mm	2	1,100	141 at 15,000 ft	216 at 15,000 ft	317	German

Type	Armament	Crew	Bomb-load (lbs)	Economical Speed (knots)	Maximum Speed (knots)	Endurance Range (sea miles)	Nationality
Ju 88 Twin Engine Monoplane	7 × 7.9mm 1 × 20mm	4	2,200	171 at 16,400 ft	260 at 14,000 ft	1,150	German
He III Twin Engine Monoplane	7 × 7.9mm 2 × 20mm	5 or 6	2,200	159 at 17,000 ft	211 at 14,000 ft	1,330	German
Ju 52 Three Engine Monoplane	5 × 7.9mm	2	5,000 (freight)	116 at sea level	145 at sea level	466 to 695	German
Cant. Z. 506 Three Engine Seaplane	1 × 12.7mm 3 × 7.7mm	4 or 5	1,750	123 at 13,000 ft	202 at 13,000 ft	1,000	Italian
S79 Three Engine Monoplane	3 × 12.7mm 2 × 7.7mm	4 or 5	2,750 or Torpedo	137 at 13,000 ft	224 at 13,000 ft	1,050	Italian

Class	Fuel (tons)	speed	*Economical*		*Moderate Despatch* 20%			*With Despatch* 60%			*Full Authorised* 100%		
			tons/ hr	range	speed	tons/ hr	range	speed	tons/ hr	range	speed	tons/ hr	range
G	455	12	1.54	3,370	19	3.7	2,380	26	7.0	1,600	31	1.32	1,180
H	455	14	1.8	3,360	20	3.6	2,400	26	6.9	1,630	31	12.0	1,120
I	455	14	1.85	3,290	19.7	3.54	2,450	26.5	7.5	1,570	31	11.9	1,130
ILEX	455	14	1.84	3,290	19.7	3.54	2,440	26.5	8.7	1,300	30.5	12.5	1,050
J/K	490	13	2.0	3,020	20	3.85	2,420	28	8.6	1,520	33	14.7	1,040

It will be seen from the tables that the endurance range for destroyers at 'full authorised' speed was only about 1,000 miles, compared with 3,000 miles at 'economical' speed. Hence, whereas at continuous economical speed the endurance was ten days, it would drop to $1\frac{1}{2}$ days at continuous full authorised speed. The problem of destroyer endurance is more fully realised when one considers a passage from Alexandria round the island of Crete and back again, which is about 900 miles. A destroyer could steam such a distance at full speed with only fuel for a further 100 miles remaining.

APPENDIX K

Honours and Awards

It is not easy to devise a specific list of the honours for a particular operation, since they were often awarded for an accumulation of instances of outstanding performance and gallantry. The following list, mainly extracted from the fourth supplement to the *London Gazette* for December 2nd, 1941, appears to apply mainly to Crete, but may be incomplete.

Victoria Cross (Posthumous)
  Petty Officer A. E. Sephton (*Coventry*)

Albert Medal (Posthumous)
  Commander W. R. Marshall-A'Deane, DSO, DSC (*Greyhound*)

Conspicious Gallantry Medal
  Marine F. Thomas (*Coventry*)

Officer of the British Empire
  Cdr P. C. L. Yorke (*Formidable*)

Distinguished Service Cross (Second Bar)
  Lt (A) P. D. J. Sparke, DSC (*Formidable*)

Distinguished Service Cross (Bar)
  Lt-Cdr (E) D. F. H. Chandler, DSC (*Isis*)
  Lt C. L. Round-Turner, DSC (*Defender*)

Distinguished Service Cross
  Lt A. P. Culmer (*Auckland*)
  Surgeon-Lt B. Crawshaw (*Grimsby*)
  Lt-Cdr R. Rhoades, RAN (*Vendetta*)
  Lt R. Hart (*Hasty*)
  Lt (E) P. G. Fyers Turner (*Defender*)
  Lt H. D. Hartnoll, RM (*Coventry*)
  Lt H. W. Barnett (*Formidable*)
  Lt R. S. Henley (*Formidable*)
  Lt (A) P. W. V. Massy (*Formidable*)
  Lt (A) A. J. Sewell, RNVR (*Formidable*)
  Sub-Lt (A) N. Cullen (*Formidable*)

Distinguished Service Medal
  Leading Seaman H. T. Hiscutt (*Auckland*)
  Leading Supply Assistant J. F. Dean (*Auckland*)
  Able Seaman A. H. Stuckey (*Auckland*)
  Chief ERA N. P. Wilkerson (*Flamingo*)
  PO E. Jackson (*Hasty*)
  Yeoman G. Bookless (*Janus*)
  Stoker PO A. E. Heath (*Isis*)

Stoker T. Duffy	(*Isis*)
ERA R. G. R. Field	(*Defender*)
Able Seaman S. G. B. Fisher	(*Coventry*)
PO J. Kemp	(*Formidable*)
PO W. Ashton	(*Formidable*)
Ordnance Artificer L. G. Sangster	(*Formidable*)
Leading Airman C. Hearnshaw	(*Formidable*)
Able Seaman S. Huntrods	(*Formidable*)
Wireman J. Menzies	(*Formidable*)

Mentioned in Despatches (Posthumous)

Able Seaman G. Stephen	(*Auckland*)
PO Cook H. Morgan	(*Grimsby*)
Lt J. H. Shears	(*Formidable*)
Sub-Lt (A) E. J. H. Dixon, RNVR	(*Formidable*)

Mentioned in Despatches

Lt (E) C. L. Meadley	(*Auckland*)
Surgeon-Lt C. J. Robarts	(*Auckland*)
Stoker PO W. Stubbings	(*Auckland*)
Stoker C. J. F. Froud	(*Auckland*)
Lt-Cdr F. D. Brown	(*Grimsby*)
Chief Stoker W. E. McFarlane	(*Grimsby*)
LSBA A. L. Porter	(*Grimsby*)
Stoker T. E. Henry	(*Grimsby*)
Joiner M. Waite	(*Grimsby*)
Cdr E. K. le Mesurier, MVO	(*Formidable*)
Lt-Cdr C. L. G. Evans, DSO, DSC	(*Formidable*)
Lt A. J. Wright, RM	(*Formidable*)
Lt E. S. Jeffs, RNVR	(*Formidable*)
Mr (Gunner) J. J. C. Fry	(*Formidable*)
Leading Seaman H. M. Gravelle	(*Formidable*)
Leading Seaman S. J. Miles	(*Formidable*)
Lt-Cdr J. P. Scatchard	(*Kashmir*)
Leading Seaman J. J. Wray	(*Kashmir*)
Able Seaman J. D. McRitchie	(*Kashmir*)
Lt A. V. Turner, RNVR	(*Janus*)
ERA W. Boddy	(*Janus*)
Able Seaman D. W. R. Davis	(*Janus*)
Sub-Lt F. H. Colenutt, RNVR	(*Glengyle*)

PO T. R. Alderson   (*Defender*)
PO T. Bodfield   (*Defender*)
Chief Shipwright S. G. Eburne   (*Defender*)
Chief Stoker T. Charnock   (*Isis*)
ERA R. W. Wilson   (*Isis*)
PO R. Bidgood   (*Coventry*)
PO C. H. J. Goldring   (*Coventry*)
Telegraphist W. L. Jackson   (*Coventry*)

Bibliography

The author is indebted for help received from the Public Record Office; the Naval Historical Branch, Admiralty; from the Britannia RN College library; and for the privilege of quoting extracts from the following marked thus ★.

In addition to the author's personal experience at the Battle for Crete, and other eye-witness accounts, the following published material has been consulted.

Admiralty Account, *The Mediterranean Fleet 1941 to 1943*. HMSO, 1944.

de Belot, R., *The Struggle for the Mediterranean 1939–1945*. Princeton Univ Press, 1951.

Bragadin, M. A., *The Italian Navy in World War II 1940–1943*. United States Naval Institute, 1957.★

Brown, J. D., *Carrier Operations in World War II*, Vol 1. Ian Allan, 1968.

Buckley, C., *Greece and Crete*. HMSO, 1952.

Clark, A., *The Fall of Crete*. Anthony Blond, 1962.

Cunningham, Viscount, of Hyndhope, *A Sailor's Odyssey*. Hutchinson, 1951.★

Fraccaroli, A., *Italian Warships of World War II*. Ian Allan, 1968.

Hodgkinson, Lieut-Cdr Hugh, *Before the Tide Turned*. Harrap, 1944.★

Lenton, H. T., and Colledge, J. J., *Warships of World War II*. Ian Allan, 1964.

Macintyre, Donald, *The Battle for the Mediterranean*. Batsford, 1964.

Pack, S. W. C., *Night Action off Cape Matapan*. Ian Allan, 1972.

Pack, S. W. C., *Sea Power in the Mediterranean*. Arthur Barker, 1971.

Playfair, I. S. O., *The Mediterranean and Middle East*, Vol II. HMSO, 1956.

Roskill, S. W., *The War at Sea*, Vol I. HMSO, 1961.

Stewart, I. McD. G., *The Struggle for Crete*. Oxford U.P., 1966.

Index

144